ERPsim

SAP Labs and Textbook

Third Edition

For Courses Utilizing

HEC Montréal's

ERPsim

Manufacturing Game

Tim Rutherford, MBA

ERPsim

SAP Labs and Textbook

Third Edition

Tim Rutherford, MBA

Written, designed, and self-published by Tim Rutherford.

Visit www.TheCourseWebsite.com for video lectures, demonstration videos, additional course and textbook resources, and updated information.

Visit Tim Rutherford's professional profile at his LinkedIn Page:

linkedin.com/in/timrutherford/

ISBN-13: 978-1074624552

ISBN-10: 1074624556

Independently published

To Sara, Lucy, and Natalie who supported me over the years
as I worked to create and complete this textbook.

*Special thank you to my UW-Milwaukee Summer 2019
BusAdmin 576 class who had the pleasure of being my
"guinea pigs" as I worked through this third edition.*

II

Note to Instructors and Students
About This Textbook

ERPsim's Manufacturing Game provides an opportunity for students of all backgrounds to learn about business through ERP. This textbook has been used as part of introductory business courses all the way up through MBA capstone courses. Those with limited business knowledge can *experience* business before they learn about it. Students with a great deal of business knowledge and experience can focus on strategic management.

While much of this textbook focuses on learning "ERP for Competitive Advantage", there's another opportunity to learn more about something SAP specific: the ECC to S/4 HANA migration. This textbook includes discussions about this migration, but, these S/4 HANA and SAP Fiori discussions are modular in nature and can be skipped without issue.

The overall objectives for this textbook are to focus on the typical end-user of an ERP system. That is, someone who does not need to know, nor need to perform, the technical side of an ERP system. The majority of business students, as an example, have no reason to learn ERP history, terminology, database design, implementation details, nor any other technical details. When they get into the "real world", they need to quickly and effectively do their task; someone else takes care of the technical details.

With that in mind, the suggested curriculum for this textbook uses SAP as an interface to operate and control a profitable organization. It's general business information; processes and strategy—ERP for Competitive Advantage.

Please note that this is meant to be a "supplemental" textbook. It's meant to supplement learning about other business concepts (which may be taught as part of your course or are pre-requisites to your course). It is also supplemental and complimentary to ERPsim's existing learning materials. In particular, students and instructors should familiarize themselves with the ERPsim Manufacturing Game Participant's Guide for the current ERPsim release.

Not only will the Participant's Guide provide additional information (such as discussions on credit ratings and details of the production process), it will also keep you informed of changes to the simulation which may have taken place since the publishing of this textbook. The Manufacturing Game Participant's Guide is updated and published before every Fall release of the ERPsim Manufacturing Game.

I hope that you, and your class, find this textbook informative. For more information, or to contact the author, visit www.TheCourseWebsite.com.

Thank you for purchasing this textbook and for reading this section.

Table of Contents

Part III

Part IV

Part I

Intro to ERP,

SAP Navigation,

and

SAP Labs

Section 01 - What is ERP?

Enterprise Resource Planning

ERP is *"Enterprise Resource Planning"*. "ERP", within this textbook, refers to a single software system utilized by an entire organization to manage all aspects of the organization. This software isn't productivity software (like a word processor or spreadsheet) but the software that runs an organization.

A well-integrated ERP system manages all functional areas: Sales/Marketing, Operations and Supply Chain Management (OSCM), Accounting/Finance, and Human Resources (HR) [or more!]. This allows everyone from an entry-level Customer Service Representative (CSR) up to the C-Level executives to have real-time access to all necessary and relevant information that is of value to their role within the organization.

This complete data integration allows for more accurate and timely information, which helps managers more quickly and more accurately make decisions for the organization. In addition, this information makes each individual's tasks more efficient as they have access to relevant information from all functional areas—right there in the single ERP system.

As a result of this single ERP system, improvements in decision making—and—customer service are possible. With a well-integrated and well-utilized ERP system, the entire organization becomes more efficient, and more profitable.

What If An Organization Doesn't Have ERP?

The good news is that an organization without ERP is not doomed to failure. There are many successful organizations without a single ERP software system. However, an argument could be made that all organizations would benefit from a well-integrated all-encompassing single ERP system.

ERP in Action: How Customers Benefit from ERP

Using a CSR (Customer Service Representative) as an example, presume that a customer calls to place an order. That customer will likely want to know if the product they are purchasing is in-stock, and how quickly the product will be shipped. If the customer has a line-of-credit with the company, they may want information on their available credit. Without one common ERP software system across the organization, the CSR may not have this information available in "real-time".

CSR Example – Taking an Order Within an ERP System

Taking this scenario to its fullest—what if the customer calls and needs to order a specific quantity of finished goods? They'll want to know the exact price for that quantity and if it's available in stock. Just to make it more complicated, they need to know the exact weight for the shipped product.

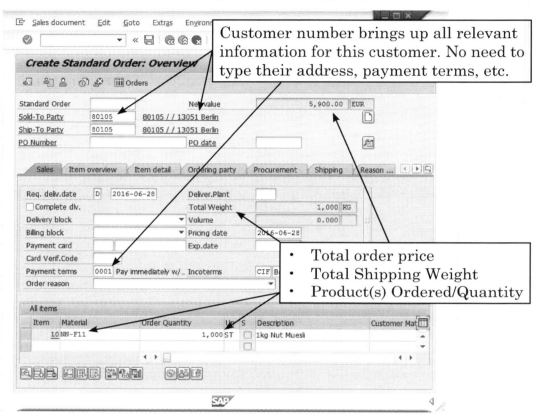

Within the above example ERP Sales Order screen, the CSR has access to company-wide information that is relevant to the customer's order.

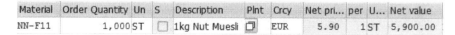

Material	Order Quantity	Un	S	Description	Plnt	Crcy	Net pri...	per	U...	Net value
NN-F11	1,000	ST	☐	1kg Nut Muesli ☐		EUR	5.90	1	ST	5,900.00

For this order, the price is simply Quantity 1,000 * 5.90, the standard price for this product. This pricing is set by another department—perhaps marketing, perhaps a sales team. The CSR does not need to know *who* created the pricing structure, but simply what the price is and how it was calculated.

> Depending on how the system is configured, the CSR may have access to discounts or other alternate pricing structures. Access to data is controlled by those who design and implement the system. In this example, the CSR is given one price with no discounts or options.

While on the phone with the customer, the CSR can also check the product's stock. No need to call the warehouse, or access a separate system, just click a button. This is referred to as "Available to Promise" or ATP.

Depending on how the ERP system is configured, the CSR may only see what is available in stock, or they may see the production orders with estimates of when the product will be available. This information is important as the CSR will be able to tell the customer when they can expect shipment of their order.

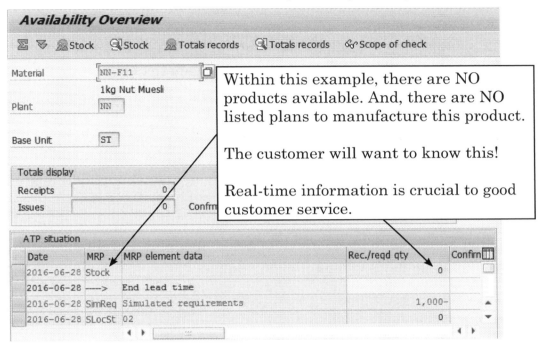

(For more details, the sales order process is completed within SAP Lab 02.)

What Makes ERP Data Available in "Real-Time"?

A well implemented ERP system incorporates all functional areas within an organization. Information from one area, one department, one employee, is available to all other areas, departments, and employees who would benefit from that information. This information becomes available across the organization due to ERP using a common database, or collection of company-wide data. One ERP system, or software package, with a *common database* allows all relevant information from all areas of the organization to be available to all areas of the organization that may need it.

In SAP, data that doesn't change often is referred to as "Master Data". But master data does more than just hold information—among other things, it could control who can see the data, how much of the data they can see, and who can change the data. Properly designed, planned, and configured master data is at the core of a proper SAP implementation.

Why is ERP Integral to a Successful Strategy?

Simply: decision making and customer service.

There are two overall strategies within any organization:

Low-Cost – Having the lowest-priced product or service on the market. Generally, this strategy involves finding a commodity item, standardizing it, procuring the lowest-cost raw materials, the least expensive labor, and/or the most cost-effective means of distribution. Ultimately, this strategy offers a product or service that meets the needs of most individuals, with the lowest price on the market.

Personalized / Customized – Having a product or service that fits exactly what the customer wants. Most times this product or service is *not* the least expensive product on the market. It's, generally, a made-to-order product or service following the customer's specifications or requirements.

Of course, somewhere in-between is where most organizations find themselves: somewhat customized, at a reasonable price. Both are customer-oriented. Both require nimble decision making.

A common database helps to successfully (profitably) execute either strategy.

If there is lag-time between the transfer of information from one area to another, overall processes are less efficient. A well implemented organization-wide ERP system allows for all relevant information to be easily accessible, which ultimately makes processes more efficient, and improves the customer's experience.

A happy customer makes for a more profitable organization.

A handful of popular ERP systems include: Microsoft Dynamics, Netsuite, IFS ERP, Epicor, OpenPRO, and, this textbook's ongoing example, SAP ERP.

Future Sections: The ECC to S/4 HANA Migration

If you work for a company that uses SAP, or, hope to work for a company that uses SAP, the ECC to S/4 HANA migration will be part of your career.

This textbook will discuss this migration as it applies to the typical business end-user. While it might "get technical", it will not be technical in nature.

If information about this migration is outside of your course's scope, the migration information can be skipped without issue.

Section 02 - S/4 HANA

The ECC to S/4 HANA Migration

This migration is "kind of a big deal".

Some are comparing this migration to the migration from MS DOS to MS Windows experienced during the 1990s. Given the time-frame for this mandatory migration, others are comparing it to Y2K.

These comparisons are as accurate as they are inaccurate. Any debate over this last statement can be made between (nerdy) intellectuals. For the purposes of this book, the migration is "kind of a big deal".

Why is the Migration Happening?

Without getting too technical, the "old" SAP ERP (ECC) is largely based on software and hardware from the 1970s. While those technologies improved in performance over the years, they reached a natural "end". The only way to improve performance was to re-write SAP ERP to meet the technologies of the 21st Century. The "new" SAP ERP (S/4 HANA) uses the latest database and hardware technologies to drive performance.

The migration is taking place because SAP is unable to continue supporting both the "old" software and the new systems. A quick Google search will show you the "end of life" for SAP ECC, which has already begun. Organizations must migrate to S/4 HANA or they will lose support from SAP.

What Does This Migration Mean for ME?

For the most part, this migration will take place "behind the scenes". Meaning, the technical staff and consultants will be making and experiencing most of the changes. That said, there are some minor to major changes that will impact the standard user of SAP. Yes, "minor to major" means the migration may not impact your SAP experience at all, or, it will impact it quite a bit.

Who Will Experience the Biggest Impact from the Migration?

Because the ERP software has been re-written, SAP took this opportunity to update and streamline several tasks and processes. For many, their tasks won't change. For others, their tasks will change quite a bit. In particular, SAP has updated its finance module. Details on these changes are outside the scope of this textbook (check sap.com for details!). More important for the average end user is the end user experience, the "UX".

For many who use SAP ERP on a daily basis, their data interface has been through the SAP GUI (pronounced "gooey"), or Graphical User Interface. For many younger users, the GUI seems like a "step back in time". And, indeed, the SAP GUI hasn't changed much over the years.

Comparing the SAP GUI *Financial Statements* selection screen between the old "Classic Theme" to the new (and S/4 enhanced) "Belize Theme":

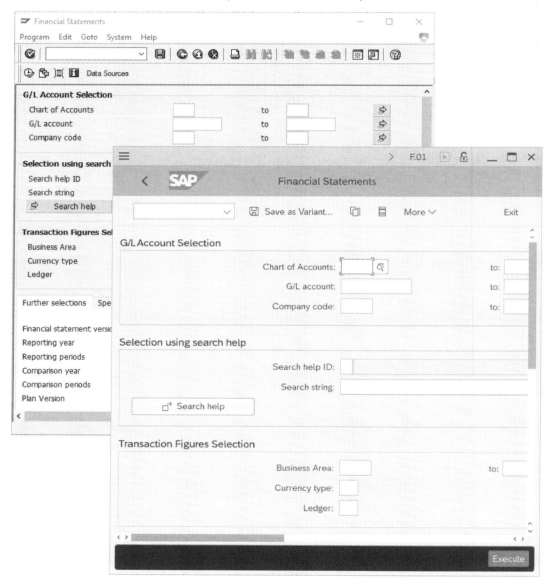

There are differences, including "easier to read" fonts, a less "blocky" design, fewer buttons, better placed buttons, and more. Yet, the SAP GUI from 10

years ago is fairly similar to the "latest and greatest" SAP GUI.

But, that's not what SAP wants you to consider. The SAP GUI has already started its "end of life" and will soon no longer be supported.

What is SAP talking about when they are considering the user experience?

SAP Fiori: The New SAP Interface

The SAP GUI is software. And while there is a "Web GUI", it's essentially the SAP GUI by way of a web browser. SAP Fiori, however, is totally different.

While Fiori is web-based, it's more like "web applications" for each task an end-user may perform. And, because it's web-based, the display options and data overlay options are nearly unlimited.

Continuing with the *Financial Statements* example, here's that same selection screen as seen using the Chrome Browser and the Fiori dashboard:

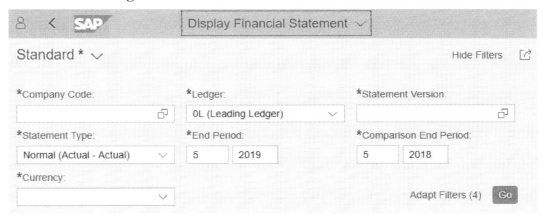

Comparing this selection screen with the SAP GUI screens on the opposite page, the options are reduced to what is important for this particular user.

And that is likely the biggest difference between the SAP GUI interface and the new Fiori interface: customization. If the user doesn't need to see all of the options, fields, and buttons, don't include them!

Beyond removing unnecessary buttons and options, because Fiori is web-based and inherently "graphic", reports can go from static "text only" lists to visualizations.

On the next page you will see the standard SAP GUI sales report compared with that same sales report within the SAP Fiori.

Can you spot the difference?

Customer Reference	Material	Σ OrdQty	Σ NV (Item)
500g Blueberries muesli	CC-F02	476	2,013.48
	CC-F02 🖭 ▪	**8,411** ▪	**35,578.53**
500g Blueberries mue... 🖭		▪ ▪ **8,411**	▪ ▪ **35,578.53**
500g Nuts muesli	CC-F01	534	2,136.00
		514	2,056.00
	CC-F01 🖭 ▪	**1,048** ▪	**4,192.00**
500g Nuts muesli 🖭		▪ ▪ **1,048**	▪ ▪ **4,192.00**
500g Raisins muesli	CC-F04	614	2,327.06
		512	1,940.48
		489	1,853.31
		475	1,800.25
		510	1,932.90
	CC-F04 🖭 ▪	**2,600** ▪	**9,854.00**
500g Raisins muesli 🖭		▪ ▪ **2,600**	▪ ▪ **9,854.00**

It's not hard to tell which display is both intuitive and easier to read.

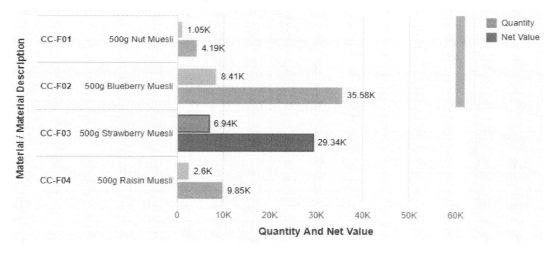

The top screen shot is the standard SAP GUI and the bottom is SAP Fiori. It's the same data in both, but the Fiori results are inherently visual.

SAP Fiori is Inherently Visual

For years, neuropsychologists have studied and proven that the human brain processes, interprets, and more effectively learns from visualizations. Look again at the example sales reports above. Start with the SAP GUI report. Which of the listed products has the highest total sales? Now look at the Fiori visualization of that same data. Your eyes probably move to the **500g**

Blueberry Muesli with its visual bar chart. The value doesn't matter, you can see the the blueberry bar chart is longest.

"Built in" and Customizable Visualizations

While the sales report is set to default to "Bar Chart", without exporting to visualization software, you can change the visualization to many different standard visualizations:

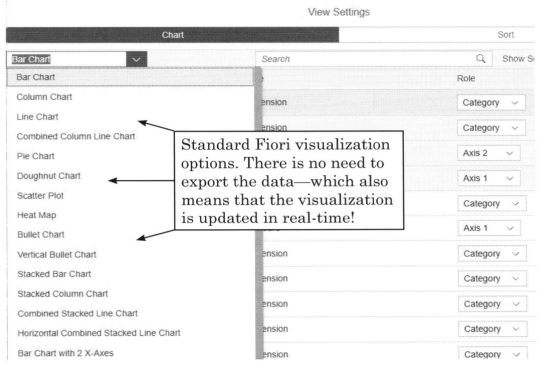

Just like other software with intuitive visualization options, SAP Fiori's reports can be filtered and adjusted:

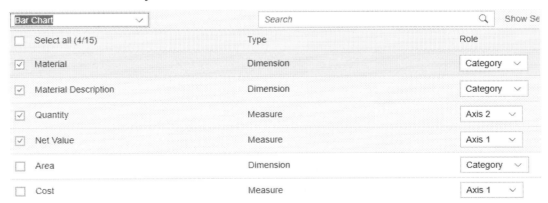

Add or remove fields, adjust how they are displayed, and, where they are displayed within the visualization.

But, this is just Fiori's built-in features. Because it is web-based, and inherently visual, SAP Fiori offers unlimited customization AND data overlay. If a Sales Manager wants to plot customers on a map based on total volume—Fiori can be customized to show them that exact information. Any data within the S/4 HANA ERP system can be displayed however the end user or manager would like to see it.

These Fiori customizations are outside the scope of this textbook. However, information about these customizations are available. Check the ERPsim website for information on Fiori customizations.

S/4 HANA and Real-Time Analytics

While SAP Fiori offers the ability to customize visualizations of data, what if you need a "ad hoc" non-standard report? What if you're not sure which data you'll need for a report? Or, the data changes over time and can't be "programmed" into SAP Fiori?

Because of changes to the HANA database, analytics is easier than ever. ERPsim provides a fantastic opportunity to implement prescriptive, predictive, and descriptive analytics—in real time.

While a "real world" installation of S/4 HANA wouldn't let just *any user* have access to all available data, ERPsim's S/4 HANA provides easy access to ALL data within the ERP system.

How do you access all of this ERPsim data? OData.

Within a later section, we'll discuss both downloading data and creating a real-time S/4 HANA server connection. This will be helpful within courses that are using the SAP GUI, but, also want to run analytics. It will allow courses that are using SAP Fiori to access data not available within the Fiori interface.

The ECC to S/4 HANA Migration

As of this textbook publication, support for the current SAP GUI ends December 2022. If you're taking this course before support ends, and, you expect to use SAP professionally, it's quite possible that you'll start working within ECC and will be part of the migration to S/4 HANA.

This migration is a huge initiative, and, will require a great deal of change management. Users unfamiliar with S/4 HANA and Fiori may be resistant to this change. After working through this textbook, you will see the benefits of the migration and can be an active agent for positive change.

This textbook will simulate the migration—starting with the SAP GUI.

Pre-Lab: Logging on to SAP

Before You Log On

In order to log on to SAP, you will need a fair amount of information. While it seems challenging right now, it will be easier once you've logged on a few times. Let's start by getting your specific information.

In one way or another, your instructor will need to provide you with either a login ID, a company letter (company code), or a product for you to manufacture. You may have a classlist or product list specific to you or your team.

The following classlist includes all of the required information:

	Roster Name	Signature	Group	Co.	SimID	Material	Product
Group 1	John Lennon	Your Group Number	1	A	A1	AA-F01	Nut
	George Harrison	Your Company Letter ($)		A	A2	AA-F02	Blueberry
	Paul McCartney	Your ERPsim ID ($?)			A3	AA-F03	Strawberry
	Richard Starkey	Your Product ($$-F0#)		A	A4	AA-F04	Raisin

From the above example, "A" is your company letter and, throughout ERPsim and the following labs, will be designated as "$". If you see one "$", that means your company letter or, following through with this example, "A". If you see "$$", that means "AA" (or your company letter twice). The number from your product material code will be designated as "#" throughout the following documentation. You will eventually see something like: "$$-F0#". Using the example classlist above, this would correspond to "AA-F04"—the material code for the assigned product, "Raisin".

If your instructor has assigned a company code (company letter / $) but has not specifically assigned a product for you to manufacture, that's okay. To continue with these instructions, pick a product (anything from $$-F01 through $$-F06) and stick with it.

SAP GUI Options

This textbook includes screen shots and instructions presuming that you are using the Windows-based SAP GUI. You may, however, be using the Web GUI, the Mac GUI, or even an older GUI. If that's the case, no worries. The screens might look a little different, but, the instructions and processes are all the same. If you are using the Web GUI, logging on will be a bit different. If you are using the Web GUI (provided by your instructor) move ahead to "Logging On".

For those using a different SAP GUI (such as the Mac GUI), the following instructions should be similar enough to get you logged on. If you have any issues, contact your instructor for help.

Logging On to the SAP GUI

Open the SAP GUI (Graphical User Interface). It may be on your desktop, within a folder called "Applications", or within "Programs" on the Windows Start Menu. Ask your instructor if you are unable to locate this icon.

Wherever you find it, it will look like this:

Double-click on this icon. If you are using the SAP GUI within a university computer lab, the logon screen will likely give a list of available servers/connections on the right panel.

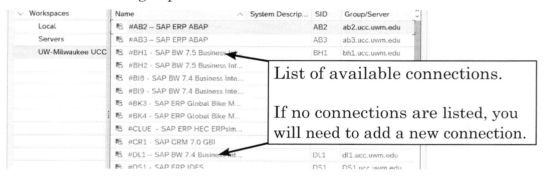

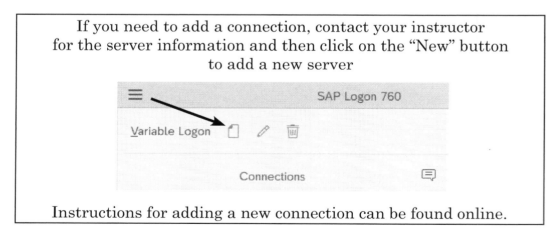

If you need to add a connection, contact your instructor for the server information and then click on the "New" button to add a new server

Instructions for adding a new connection can be found online.

The server you choose will depend on what you are doing within SAP. Contact your instructor for your server information. Typically, your instructor will provide you with this information at the start of each event requiring SAP.

Connect to Your Server

Within the SAP logon GUI, look at the list of available connections. Find the server for the client you intend to use (provided by your instructor).

Find your server within the list and double-click it.

You will see a screen similar to this:

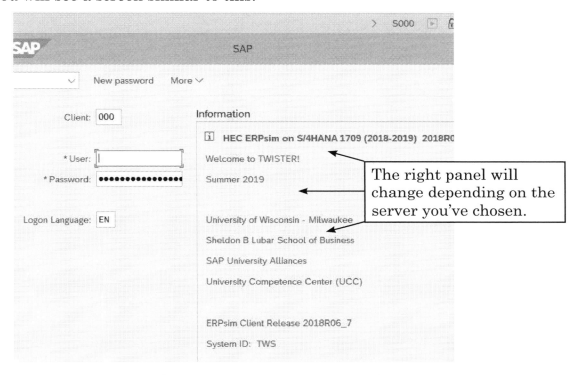

The right panel will change depending on the server you've chosen.

Add the appropriate information—provided by your instructor:

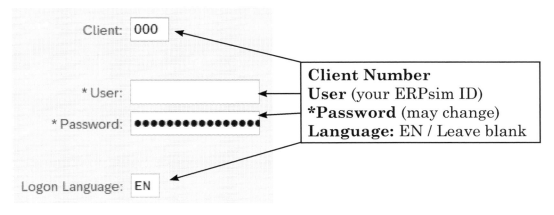

Client Number
User (your ERPsim ID)
*Password (may change)
Language: EN / Leave blank

*This is by default a temporary password.

You will probably be prompted for a new password:

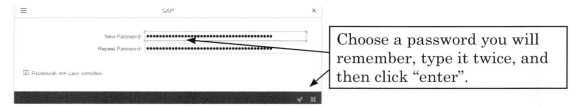

Choose a password you will remember, type it twice, and then click "enter".

Depending on how your ERPsim course is organized, you may use a client / company code once, or you may log on over and over to the same client / company code.

If you plan to log back onto the server / client / company code multiple times, it's in your best interest to use the same password each time you log on to a new server/client. And... there is absolutely no need to make the password complicated. No one will be "hacking" your SAP system. Keep it simple and memorable.

Once you've typed in a new password, several information only screens may pop up. Provided there are no error messages, just click enter until you reach a screen similar to this:

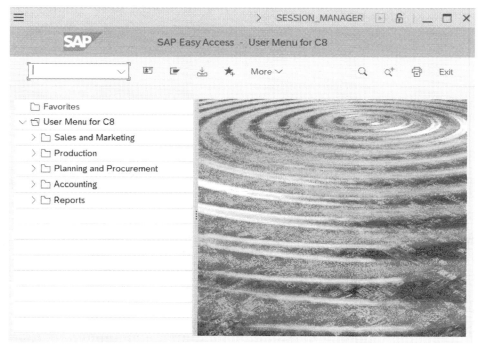

Congratulations! You've logged on to SAP!

Pre-Lab: Navigating SAP

The SAP GUI

All concepts, strategies, or processes you learn within this course are meant to be actualized and practiced within a "live" SAP system. SAP's GUI is functional and presumes that you know what you're doing. And why not? The typical SAP user only utilizes a handful of transactions/screens throughout their work day. To increase speed, SAP presumes that the user knows what they are doing. And that's true for the typical SAP user. Once you know the interface, you'll zip around from transaction to transaction.

But, if you've never used it before, it can be intimidating.

This textbook and following labs presume that you have not used the SAP GUI before. And, even if you have used it before, this section may teach you some navigation tips you don't know.

Change the SAP GUI Theme

Because we are using an S/4 HANA server with Fiori visual options, the default SAP GUI "theme" will show you some *Fioritized* visualizations. In an effort to stay "backwards compatible" with SAP ECC, whenever this textbook utilizes SAP GUI screens shots they will be *without* the Fiori visualizations. Why? If you were to begin work for a company that has not completed the migration to S/4 HANA, the lack of Fiori visualizations may leave you confused. In addition, some companies have migrated to S/4 HANA and have chosen not to use the Fiori visualizations.

With that in mind, let's change the SAP GUI's visualization to a common theme *without* Fiori visualizations. The following theme has been available since the SAP GUI 740 release and has stayed relatively constant.

To make the change to your theme, log on to your assigned SAP server, client, and user ID. (If you have questions about how to do this, go back to the previous Pre-Lab "Logging on to SAP".)

Once you are logged in, you'll need to change the "Theme Settings". Depending on which SAP GUI you have installed, you may see different options for making this change.

The following are a couple of options:

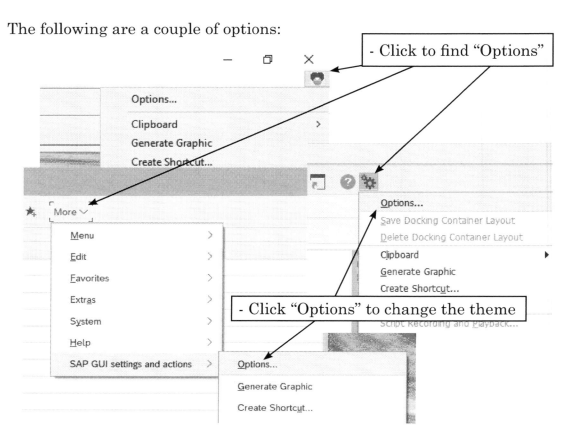

- Click to find "Options"

- Click "Options" to change the theme

Once you've found "Options", expand "Visual Design" and then click "Theme Settings". Select Theme: "Blue Crystal Theme":

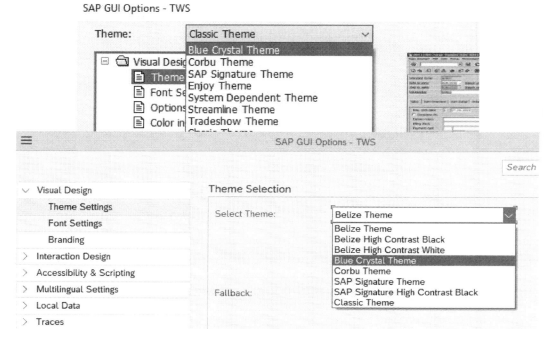

Click "Apply" and then "Ok" to change the settings.

Changes to your theme won't take place until the next time that you log on.

To match the following screen shots, log off and then log back on.

Click "Log off", or, just click the "X" to close the SAP GUI:

Click "Yes" to Log Off.

Log back on using the server, client and user ID assigned to you. Remember that if you were prompted to change the password, it is the password that you set for this user ID.

When you log back on, you'll find that the theme has been changed.

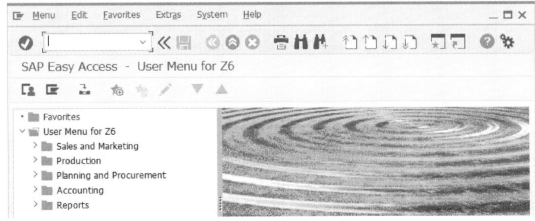

This theme will match the SAP GUI screen shots used throughout this book.

Navigation and the ERPsim Job Aid

Within this course you'll be utilizing one of the ERPsim games. These games simulate a market situation within a full-blown SAP system. Typical transactions used throughout the game are included on a separate "Job Aid" specific to the game you are playing. Your instructor will provide this for you when you are playing one of the games.

The Job Aid lists transaction codes, or T-codes, and then brief instructions. T-codes allow for quick maneuvering from transaction screen to transaction screen. If you continue to utilize the SAP GUI throughout this course, you'll likely start to memorize these T-codes.

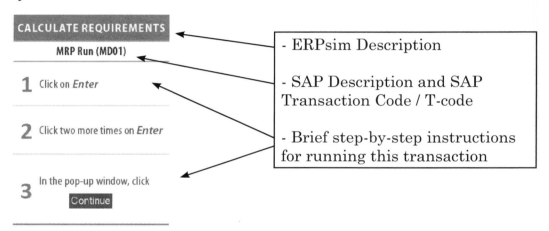

- ERPsim Description

- SAP Description and SAP Transaction Code / T-code

- Brief step-by-step instructions for running this transaction

Transaction codes are entered directly into the SAP GUI.

Enter the SAP T-Code within the SAP "Command Field"

Can't find the command field? Sometimes it's hidden.

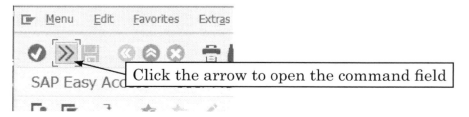

Click the arrow to open the command field

Practice: SAP Navigation

Transaction Code: CS12

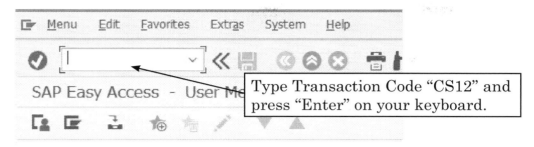

The menu screen disappears and you're within transaction "CS12".

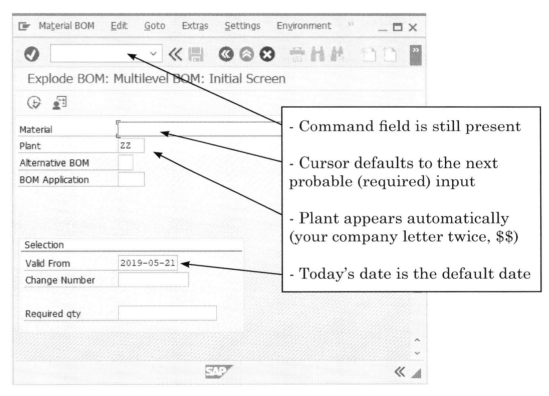

Return to the main SAP Menu by clicking the back arrow.

Let's try a different transaction.

Transaction Code: VA01

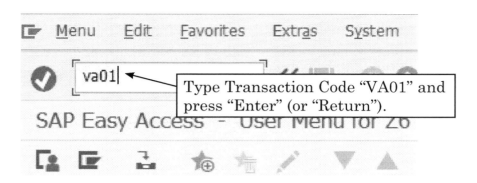

Type Transaction Code "VA01" and press "Enter" (or "Return").

As you execute the new transaction, the SAP Menu disappears.

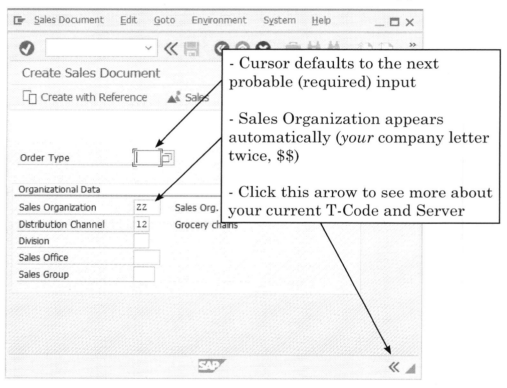

- Cursor defaults to the next probable (required) input

- Sales Organization appears automatically (*your* company letter twice, $$)

- Click this arrow to see more about your current T-Code and Server

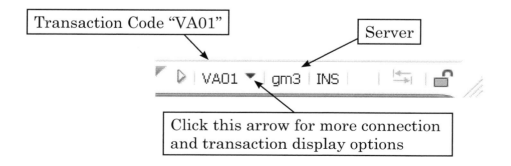

Transaction Code "VA01"

Server

Click this arrow for more connection and transaction display options

The SAP GUI allows you to interact with one transaction at a time. In order to move from one transaction to another, you have two choices:

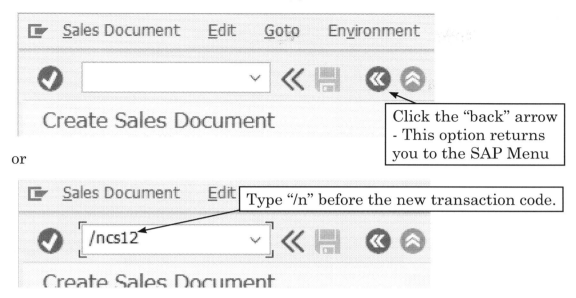

Click the "back" arrow - This option returns you to the SAP Menu

or

Type "/n" before the new transaction code.

Typing "/n" before the new transaction code tells the SAP GUI to close the current transaction and then open the new transaction. This bypasses the SAP Menu.

If you haven't already, try typing "/ncs12" into the SAP Menu's Command Field.

You should find yourself in the new transaction, CS12 "Explode BOM".

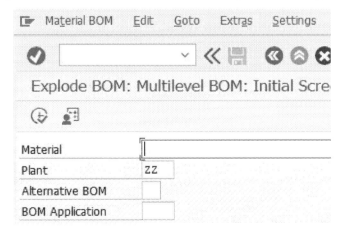

Within the Command Field, type "/nva01" to return to the "Create Sales Order" transaction.

New Sessions

Throughout the SAP Labs, and most certainly during ERPsim gameplay, you will need to have multiple windows opened at once. In order to run a new transaction – while keeping the current transaction window open – you'll have to open a new window. SAP refers to these windows as "Sessions".

To open a new window, click the "New GUI Window" button.

This opens up a whole new SAP Menu within another window.

You can also use a shortcut within the command line to run a new transaction within a new session. Try typing: /omd01

> If you are using the Web GUI and want to open a new window, copy the URL for the Web GUI and paste it into a new browser tab or window.

The SAP GUI allows each user to run SIX separate sessions/windows. As you play the ERPsim games, you'll learn which transactions are required for your specific activities, and which of those transactions should be opened in new sessions.

But wait, there's more...

This section was not meant to exhaustively cover SAP navigation but to give you enough of a background to get started in SAP. The following SAP Labs give you step-by-step instructions for navigating SAP. Read the directions carefully.

> Note: the following labs presume that you're learning as you go and that you require fewer and fewer "step-by-step" instructions. By Lab 03, it presumes you've learned the basic navigation detailed in Lab 01. Pay attention, read, and learn as you go.

Lab 01 - Production

Forecast to Finished Goods

Within this lab you will create 1,000 of your specific 500g muesli product, from nothing to something.

> ### **Important Steps *Before* You Start!**
>
> This lab presumes that you have already
>
> 1. Acquired your login information and have logged on to SAP,
>
> 2. Changed your SAP GUI theme to "Blue Crystal", and,
>
> 3. Learned basic SAP GUI Navigation techniques.
>
> If you have not, complete the pre-Labs: "Logging on to SAP" and "Navigating SAP" before you start!
>
> **Instructors: Before your students begin these labs you must log on as "admin" and run ZSIM_START to prepare the client for the Extended Manufacturing Game. This must be repeated on the 1st of the month.

First, let's determine what your product will be. Typically this is assigned to you by your instructor. If you have not been assigned a specific product, choose one! There are six 500g muesli products available for manufacture.

> $$-F01 – 500g Nut Muesli
> $$-F02 – 500g Blueberry Muesli
> $$-F03 – 500g Strawberry Muesli
> $$-F04 – 500g Raisin Muesli
> $$-F05 – 500g Original Muesli
> $$-F06 – 500g Mixed Fruit Muesli

Whether you've been assigned a product, or, you just picked one, all finished goods use the "material number" format:

$$-F0#

This is an important distinction because you need to understand the $$ and # variables to move forward. The $ is your company letter. Don't know your company letter? What's your user ID? (your login ID?) Whatever letter is in your user ID is your company letter. As an example, if you logged on using N3, the "N" is your company letter. That company letter ($) is the preface to your product's material number. Continuing with the example "N", using the format $$-F0#, your material code is NN-F0#.

What about that "#"? If you choose a product yourself, or, if you've been assigned a product, you can find that material code / number within this chart:

> $$-F01 – 500g Nut Muesli
> $$-F02 – 500g Blueberry Muesli
> $$-F03 – 500g Strawberry Muesli
> $$-F04 – 500g Raisin Muesli
> $$-F05 – 500g Original Muesli
> $$-F06 – 500g Mixed Fruit Muesli

Continuing with the "N" example, if you were assigned 500g Nut Muesli, your material code is NN-F01. If your company code is "C" and you choose 500g Raisin Muesli, your material code is CC-F04.

> ****If you are working within a group****
>
> Confirm that you aren't picking duplicate products. You don't want 3 people within the same company code all manufacturing the same product. Each person on your team should choose a different product.

If you still need some help determining your company or your product, ask a group member* or refer back to the class list (if provided by your instructor):

	Roster Name	Signature	Group	Co.	SimID	Material	Product
Group 1	John Lennon	Your Group Number	1	A	A1	AA-F01	Nut
	George Harrison	Your Company Letter ($)	1	A	A2	AA-F02	Blueberry
	Paul McCartney	Your ERPsim ID ($#)	1	A	A3	AA-F03	Strawberry
	Richard Starkey	Your Product ($$-F0#)	1	A	A4	AA-F04	Raisin

Do you have your product? Great—now let's go manufacture it!

> *Note: These labs presume that you are working within a group. If you are not, just ignore the references to your "group".

The BOM – Bill of Material

The BOM (Bill of Material) is the "ingredients list", or, the overall "recipe" for this product. Let's look at the ingredients within your product. Within all of our examples / screen shots, we will be producing "ZZ-F06", or 500g Mixed Fruit

Muesli for Company Z. Be sure to adjust the instructions to your company, your personal product, and the appropriate raw materials for your specific 500g muesli product. (Note: these labs are written for 500g products only.)

Type the following SAP Transaction Code into the SAP Command Field (refer to the pre-lab, "Navigating SAP", if you do not know how to do this):

Transaction Code: CS12

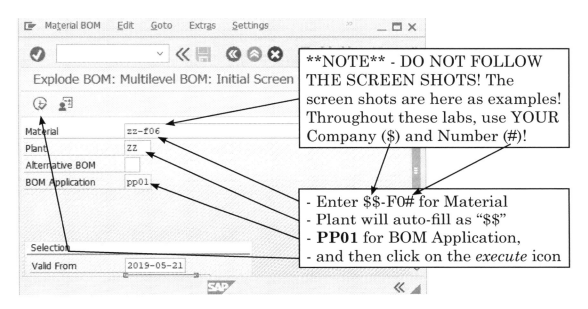

Click "enter" (⊘) if you receive the notice "...not relevant for segmentation."

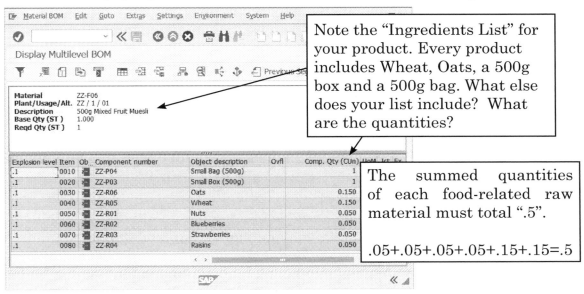

This is the Bill of Materials (BOM) or "ingredients list" for manufacturing one finished box of your assigned 500g muesli product.

For your product ($$-F0#), we want to manufacture 1,000 finished products. You will need to order enough of each ingredient/material to manufacture 1,000 finished products. How many of each listed material should you order? It's easy to calculate this. From your BOM, how many of the following ingredients are required to create 1,000 finished products?

Material ZZ-F06
Plant/Usage/Alt. ZZ / 1 / 01
Description 500g Mixed Fruit Muesli
Base Qty (ST) 1.000
Reqd Qty (ST) 1

Explosion level	Item	Ob...	Component number	Object description	Ovfl	Comp. Qty (CUn)	UoM	Ict E
.1	0010		ZZ-P04	Small Bag (500g)		1	ST	L
.1	0020		ZZ-P03	Small Box (500g)		1	ST	L
.1	0030		ZZ-R06	Oats		0.150	KG	L
.1	0040		ZZ-R05	Wheat		0.150	KG	L
.1	0050		ZZ-R01	Nuts		0.050	KG	L
.1	0060		ZZ-R02	Blueberries		0.050	KG	L
.1	0070		ZZ-R03	Strawberries		0.050	KG	L
.1	0080		ZZ-R04	Raisins		0.050	KG	L

Based on the BOM, complete the following ingredients list for 1,000 of your product:

Ingredient	Component Number	Comp. Qty	x1000	Total
Nuts			x1000	
Bluberries			x1000	
Strawberries			x1000	
Raisins			x1000	
Wheat			x1000	
Oats			x1000	
Box			x1000	
Bag			x1000	

The above chart is the "shopping list" for your product. You want to create 1,000 of your product and this is what you have to buy in order to manufacture the product.

> *Note that this is a portion of MRP—Material Requirements Planning. You'll see more of this as we start the ERPsim Manufacturing Game.

Calculate the raw material requirements for your product and let's go shopping!

Open a new session (leaving the BOM session open).

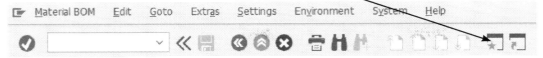

Create Purchase Order: Foodbroker Inc.

Transaction Code: ME21N

Which will bring up the following screen:

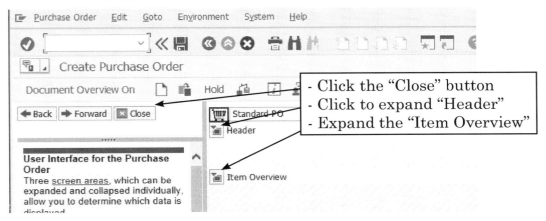

- Click the "Close" button
- Click to expand "Header"
- Expand the "Item Overview"

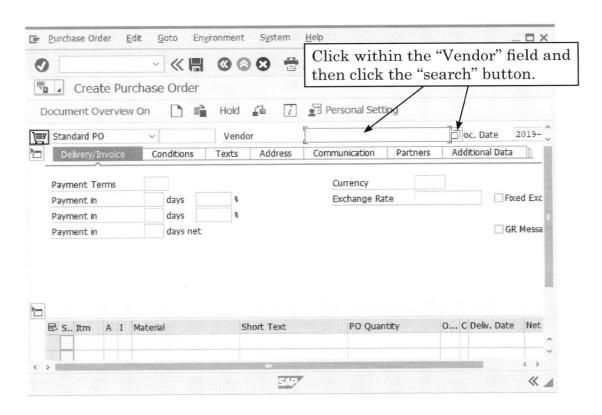

Click within the "Vendor" field and then click the "search" button.

Clicking the "search" button brings up the following screen:

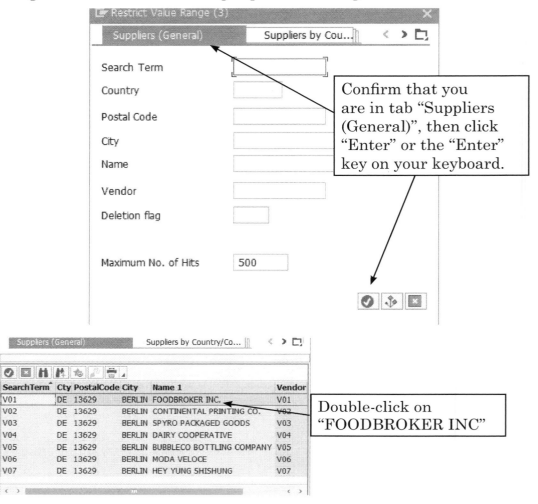

Confirm that you are in tab "Suppliers (General)", then click "Enter" or the "Enter" key on your keyboard.

Double-click on "FOODBROKER INC"

We will need to create two purchase orders (POs), one for the food materials and the other for the packaging requirements – the boxes and bags.

Double-clicking on "FOODBROKER INC.", will bring you back to the PO page.

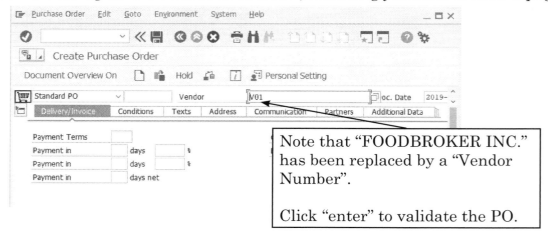

Note that "FOODBROKER INC." has been replaced by a "Vendor Number".

Click "enter" to validate the PO.

The vendor name "FOODBROKER INC." has been replaced by a vendor number. SAP utilizes a **master data record** for information that does not change that often, such as customer and vendor names and numbers. This vendor's information has been consolidated down to a simple three character code, "V01". This is consistent across all functional areas within SAP, from procurement to accounting.

After clicking "Enter", the error: "Enter Purch. Group" will display.

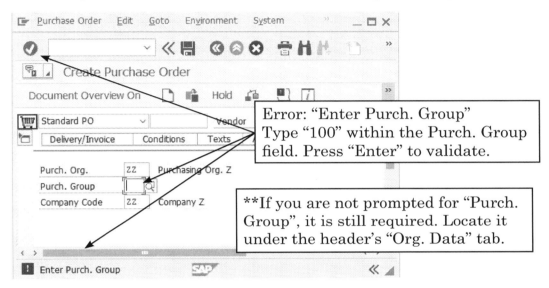

Error: "Enter Purch. Group"
Type "100" within the Purch. Group field. Press "Enter" to validate.

**If you are not prompted for "Purch. Group", it is still required. Locate it under the header's "Org. Data" tab.

Referencing your shopping list from a previous page, input your required raw materials—but only FOOD ITEMS. We'll need to create a separate PO for the boxes and bags. Be very careful to type the amounts and the "Material" EXACTLY as it is listed within the BOM. Remember that you have the BOM open in another window if you need to double-check a material code or quantity.

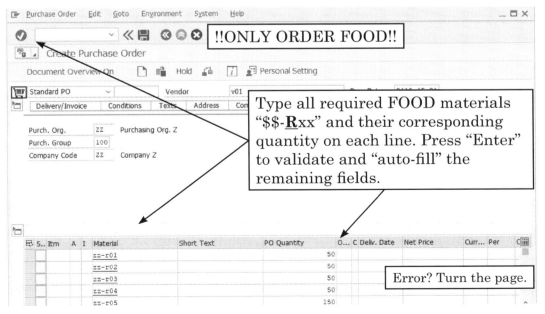

!!ONLY ORDER FOOD!!

Type all required FOOD materials "$$-Rxx" and their corresponding quantity on each line. Press "Enter" to validate and "auto-fill" the remaining fields.

Error? Turn the page.

Check for Errors!

SAP "validates" your inputs after you click "Enter". Nothing is saved. At this time, you may find some errors or automatic changes within your PO.

Right now is the time to fix all of your errors. Otherwise, you'll get further into this lab and ... your product won't be manufactured.

Items to note:

- If your order quantity doesn't match the rounding rules, it will automatically change to the rounded amount. Each raw material's master data record is set to automatically round up. This appears as a yellow "warning". The revised values will be higher than your initial amount. That's okay—too many raw materials is fine. You'll only have a problem if you have too few raw materials.

- "Can delivery date be met?" — this is just a yellow "warning". In the "real world" it's unlikely that you'd order your raw materials and receive them the same day. Feel free to ignore this warning.

- If you tried to enter —all— of the raw materials from your grocery list, you will receive an error. SAP has been programmed to know that Foodbroker Inc. does not sell boxes and bags. If you tried to order everything from your BOM at once, you received an error. While you can fix this within the PO, it's sometimes easier to just start over.

- Another common mistake comes from typing the wrong material code. The format should follow: $$-**R**0#. If you use $$-F0#, the "F" designates a finished product. You will be manufacturing your finished products, not ordering them.

What about an error not listed? Throughout this lab, and throughout the rest of your course, it will be impossible to predict all of the errors you or your group members may make. It's best to slow down, read the instructions, and be prepared to make mistakes. Yes, you will make mistakes—and that's part of learning how to navigate within SAP.

Correct any errors—if you can

Remember, you've pressed "Enter" at this point. Nothing is saved, nothing is beyond repair. If you abandon this PO without saving, nothing has happened.

Sometimes it's easier to just re-start the process rather than spend the time trying to correct or troubleshoot multiple errors.

Don't worry—it'll move more quickly the 2nd time you do this.

Within the "header", click on the tab marked "Status".

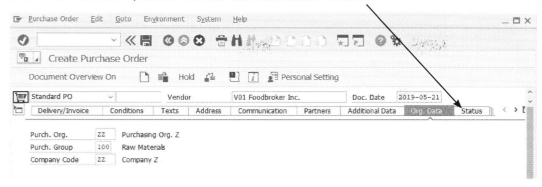

Confirm that you've ordered 500KG (or more depending on rounding).

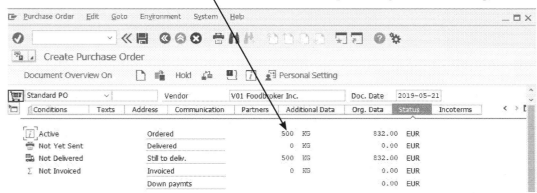

No matter what the quantities are of your finished product's BOM, the total weight of the package is 500 grams. 500 grams x 1,000 = 500 kilograms.

If your total is *below* 500 KG, double-check your inputs. An incorrect quantity here means that you will be unable to successfully complete the manufacture of your finished product.

Right now is the time to fix any mistakes. If your raw material quantities are accurate, move forward. Otherwise, keep working until your PO is correct.

If everything looks okay, take a look at the "Item Overview" .

S.. Itm	A I	Material	Short Text	PO Quantity	O...	C	Deliv. Date	Net Price	Curr...
10		ZZ-R01	Nuts	50 KG		D	2019-05-22	1.82	EUR
20		ZZ-R02	Blueberries	50 KG		D	2019-05-22	4.00	EUR
30		ZZ-R03	Strawberries	50 KG		D	2019-05-22	4.02	EUR
40		ZZ-R04	Raisins	50 KG		D	2019-05-22	1.07	EUR
50		ZZ-R05	Wheat	150 KG		D	2019-05-22	0.99	EUR
60		ZZ-R06	Oats	150 KG		D	2019-05-22	0.92	EUR

You'll see that many of the fields are "auto-populated" based on the Vendor, material code, and the quantity. This is an example of SAP master data or, in general ERP terms, the "common database". This makes an individual user's work easier as it would take a long time to type all of this information. However, with a common database, this information is auto-populated within each field.

Double-check your work. Are you sure that your quantities are correct?

This is your last chance to fix any mistakes.

> **Errors Within Your PO!**
>
> You may have noticed that the last two pages are dedicated to checking for errors. THIS is the most common place where students make mistakes.
>
> Slow down, read the instructions, check for errors. By slowing down and confirming your PO, you'll save time in the long-run.

Click on the "Conditions" tab.

Make sure that you're working within the "Headers" area of the PO.

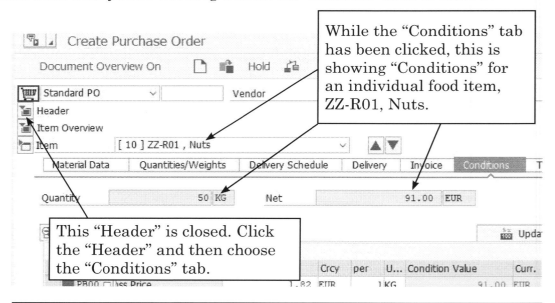

While the "Conditions" tab has been clicked, this is showing "Conditions" for an individual food item, ZZ-R01, Nuts.

This "Header" is closed. Click the "Header" and then choose the "Conditions" tab.

> There are many places to make errors within these labs. And it's impossible to predict errors you might make. If you continue to find yourself fixing errors, slow down. These step-by-step instructions give you all of the details required to complete these labs. If you're rushing through them or otherwise not paying attention to detail, you are far more error prone. Slow down—this isn't a race.

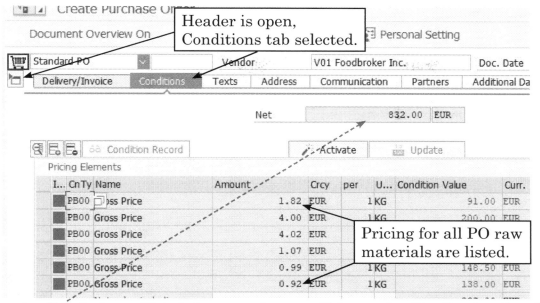

Note the "Net" above. This is how much you will be paying Foodbroker Inc. for these raw materials.

> ****The following is not "busy work" nor "information only"****
>
> Note your current page number within this lab and find the Relevant Information Form at the end of this Textbook. It should be the final page of the textbook. If you are unable to locate it, check the Table of Contents for its page number.
>
> This Relevant Information Form is used to log your lab information, either for troubleshooting or for other areas of this or future labs.
>
> In the area provided on the Relevant Information Form, write the net amount for this PO on line 1.1 and then come back to this page. The "Net" amount here will be necessary within SAP Lab 03.
>
> (Note: you're also about to write the value for line 1.2…)

This is your last chance to check this PO. If all of your numbers appear to be accurate, and you have no errors, click "Save" on the tool bar. A question box may pop up:

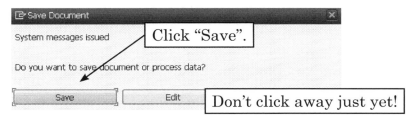

An important message will briefly appear on the bottom left corner of your SAP

This is your last chance to fix any mistakes.   33

session:

 Standard PO created under the number 4500000098

> On the *Relevant Information* Form, located at the end of this textbook, write this PO Number on line 1.2.

Do not close the "Create Purchase Order" transaction. Remember, we still need to order bags and boxes.

Create Purchase Order: Continental Printing Co.

From here, click the "vendor" search button again:

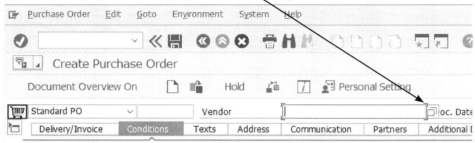

Click "Enter" on the next screen and double-click "Continental Printing Co."

Press "Enter" to start creation of your new PO for 1,000 small boxes, and 1,000 small bags. Remember that you will need to add "100" as the "Purch. Group".

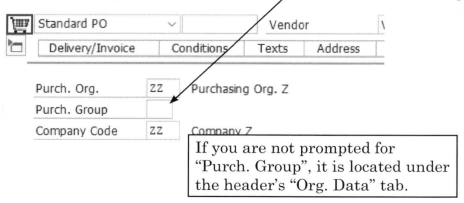

If you are not prompted for "Purch. Group", it is located under the header's "Org. Data" tab.

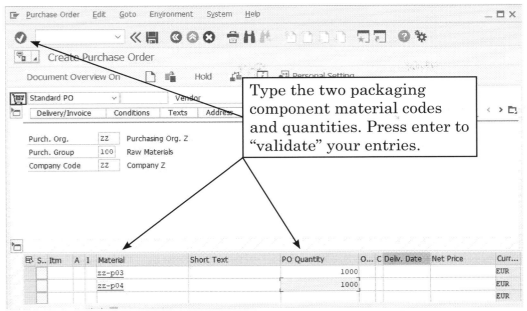

Follow the same error checking as the Foodbroker Inc. PO.

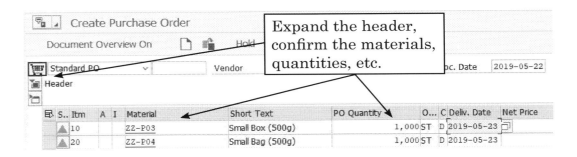

Now is the time to fix any errors you might find. Remember, if there is an error now, you will not be able to manufacture your finished good.

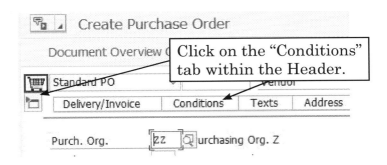

Note the "Net" amount for your PO.

Create Purchase Order: Continental Printing Co.   35

> On the *Relevant Information* Form, located at the end of
> this textbook, write this *Net Amount* on line 1.3.

Click "Save" and, if prompted, "Save" again on the "Save Document" dialogue box to save the document and process the data. Watch for your PO number.

> On the *Relevant Information* form, located at the end
> of this textbook, write this *PO Number* on line 1.4.

Click the back button until you reach the "SAP Menu".

While in "real life" it could take several weeks to receive our order, and within ERPsim it takes 1-5 simulated days to receive an order, we're going to "spoof" the system and receive materials from both POs today.

Goods Receipt: Foodbroker Inc.

We'll start with the PO from Foodbroker Inc.

From the SAP Menu,

Transaction Code: MIGO

Which will bring up the following screen:

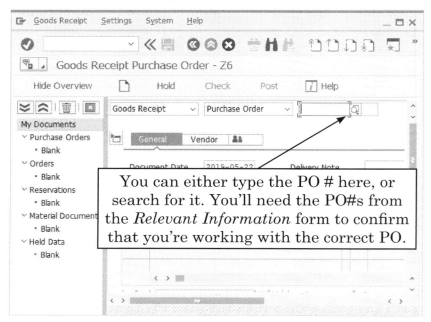

If you are searching for the PO, a search screen pops up which is similar to the vendor search screen within ME21n, Purchase Order Creation.

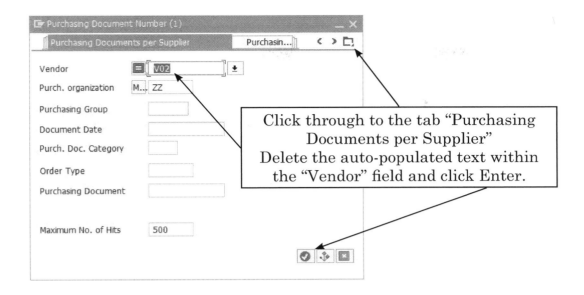

Click through to the tab "Purchasing Documents per Supplier"
Delete the auto-populated text within the "Vendor" field and click Enter.

This is searching for all POs within your company (meaning your group members). You could (and probably will) find several other POs within the search results. Double-click on the PO# from "FOODBROKER INC" which you wrote down on the *Relevant Information* Form.

DO NOT open Continental Printing's PO! One PO at a time!

Take the time to read this sentence.

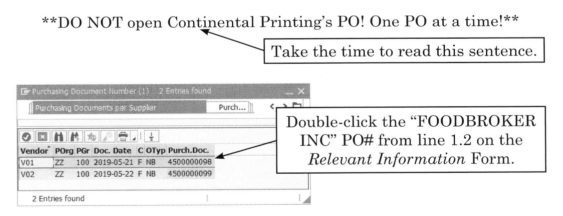

Double-click the "FOODBROKER INC" PO# from line 1.2 on the *Relevant Information* Form.

Click "Enter" to auto-populate the Goods Receipt screen with all of the items on the PO.

DO NOT open Continental Printing's PO! One PO at a time!

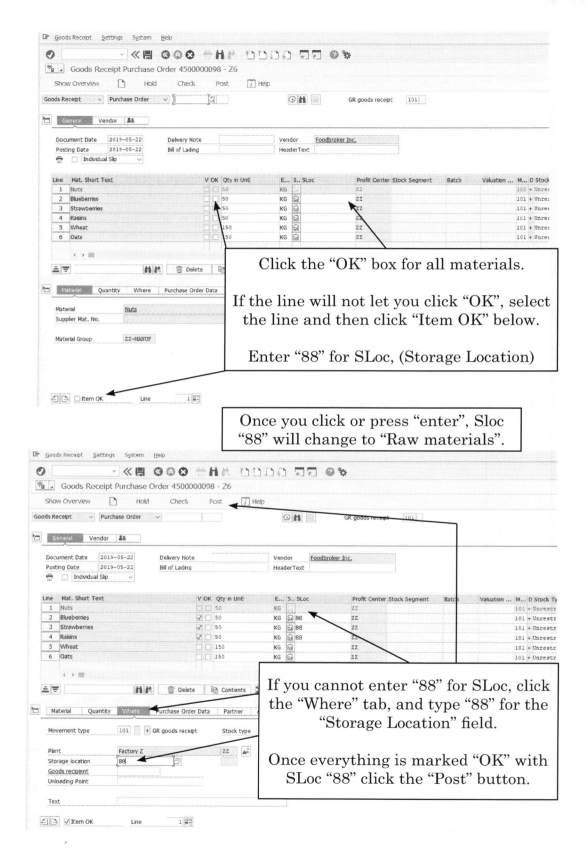

Goods Receipt: Continental Printing Co.

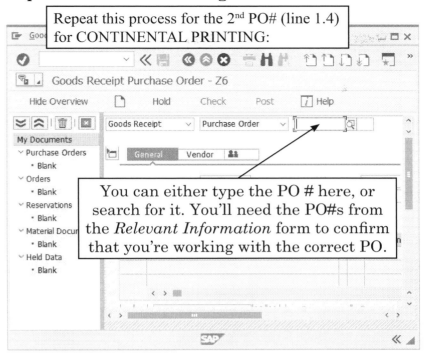

Repeat this process for the 2nd PO# (line 1.4) for CONTINENTAL PRINTING:

You can either type the PO # here, or search for it. You'll need the PO#s from the *Relevant Information* form to confirm that you're working with the correct PO.

If you are searching for the PO, a search screen pops up which is similar to the vendor search screen within ME21n, Purchase Order Creation.

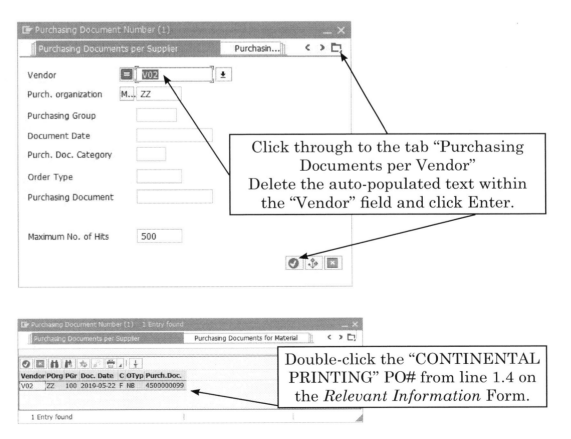

Click through to the tab "Purchasing Documents per Vendor"
Delete the auto-populated text within the "Vendor" field and click Enter.

Double-click the "CONTINENTAL PRINTING" PO# from line 1.4 on the *Relevant Information* Form.

Click "Enter" to auto-populate the Goods Receipt screen with all of the items on the Continental Printing PO.

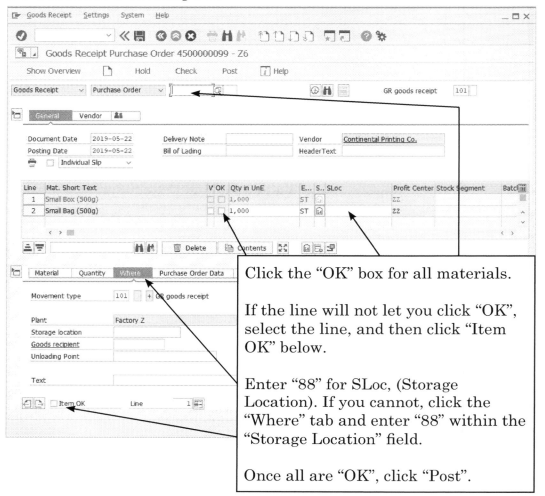

Click the "OK" box for all materials.

If the line will not let you click "OK", select the line, and then click "Item OK" below.

Enter "88" for SLoc, (Storage Location). If you cannot, click the "Where" tab and enter "88" within the "Storage Location" field.

Once all are "OK", click "Post".

After clicking "post", click the "Back" button until you reach the main SAP Menu. Confirm that your product's raw materials are now in stock by viewing the Stock/Requirements List:

Transaction Code: MD04

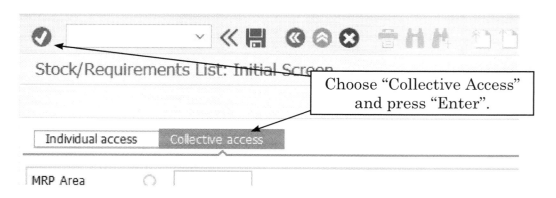

Choose "Collective Access" and press "Enter".

The Stock/Requirements List

Notice the stock of finished goods and raw materials. Recall that the rest of your group is also working on this lab. You may see your exact number of raw materials, and you may see a wide variety of raw materials. Exact completion of this lab is very important as you'll be using raw materials in stock. If you

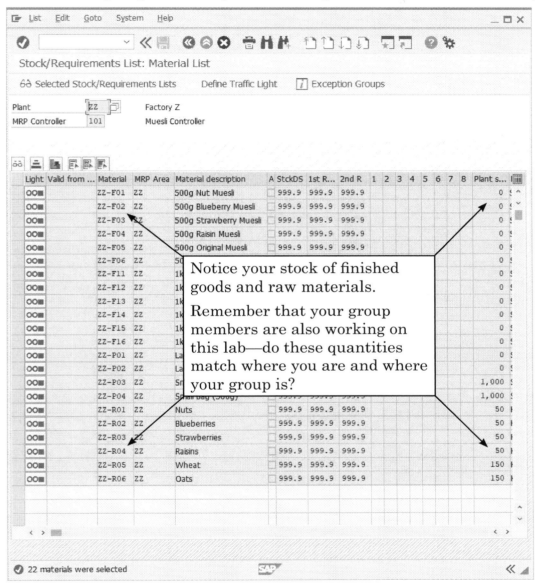

ordered too few of a raw material and your group members order the correct amount, you *could* be using their raw materials to finish your product. Confirm with your group members that these numbers are accurate. If they are not accurate, you may inadvertently throw off your group member's labs!

Before we move forward, take a look at the Stock/Requirements List. It's important that you understand what you are seeing here.

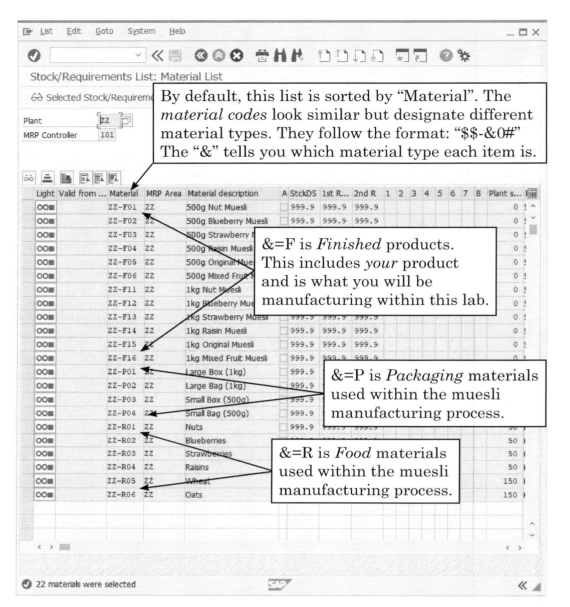

Within the Stock/Requirements list, find *your* product. Do note that your product's "Material Description" includes "500g XXXX Muesli". The Material Code includes an "F" for "Finished Product". The Material Code looks like this: "$$-**F**0#".

Within the next step of this lab, if you were to pick the *food* raw material associated with *your* finished product, you're setting up SAP to manufacture that raw material. As an example, if you pick "Raisins", "$$-**R**04", you're telling SAP that within your manufacturing plant, you'd like to manufacture raisins. Obviously no one "manufactures" raisins. Within this lab, we order raisins from Foodbroker Inc. Instead, you must pick *your* product, as an example,

"500g Raisin Muesli", material code "$$-**F**04".

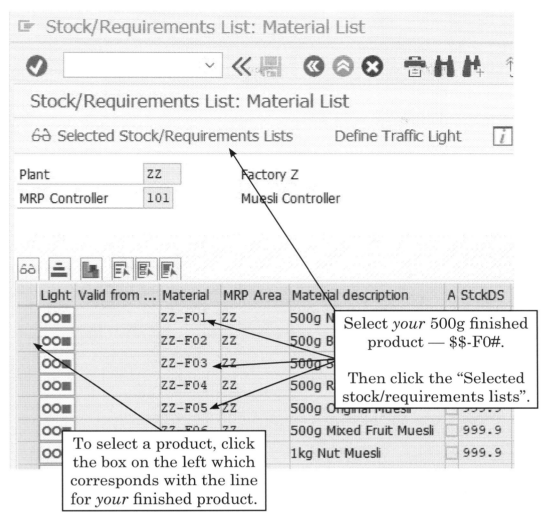

Stock/Requirements List: Material List

6a Selected Stock/Requirements Lists   Define Traffic Light   [i]

| Plant | ZZ | Factory Z |
| MRP Controller | 101 | Muesli Controller |

Light	Valid from ...	Material	MRP Area	Material description	A	StckDS
OO▣		ZZ-F01	ZZ	500g N		
OO▣		ZZ-F02	ZZ	500g B		
OO▣		ZZ-F03	ZZ	500g S		
OO▣		ZZ-F04	ZZ	500g R		
OO▣		ZZ-F05	ZZ	500g Original Muesli		999.9
OO▣		ZZ-F06	ZZ	500g Mixed Fruit Muesli		999.9
OO▣				1kg Nut Muesli		999.9

Select *your* 500g finished product — $$-F0#.

Then click the "Selected stock/requirements lists".

To select a product, click the box on the left which corresponds with the line for *your* finished product.

The Stock/Requirements List is specific to your product and shows your available quantity.

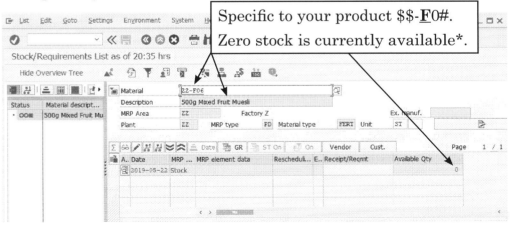

Specific to your product $$-**F**0#.

Zero stock is currently available*.

*Do you have stock? Confirm that you're using the correct material code. Did you already complete this lab? What else may have happened? Before you move forward figure out why you have stock.

Create Planned Order

We'll refer back to this Stock/Requirements List, so leave it open.

Open a new session. (Try using /omd11 in the command field!)

Transaction Code: MD11

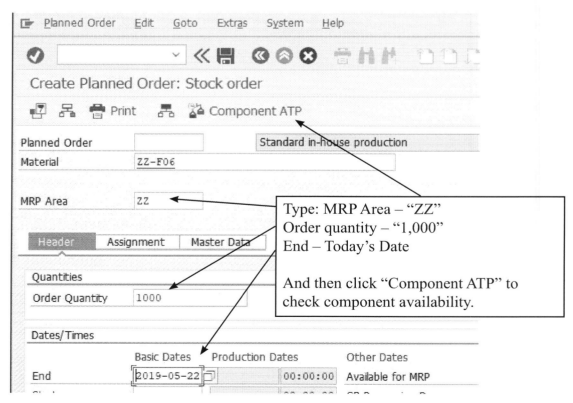

This ATP (Available to Promise) check looks at the BOM and your Order Quantity and then confirms that you have enough raw materials in stock to complete this Production Order.

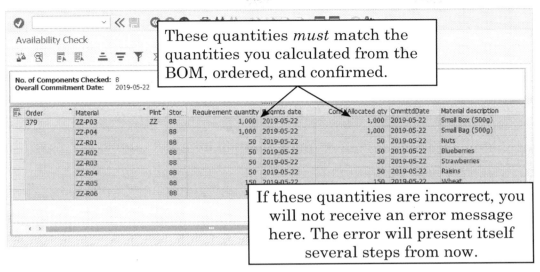

These quantities *must* match the quantities you calculated from the BOM, ordered, and confirmed.

If these quantities are incorrect, you will not receive an error message here. The error will present itself several steps from now.

If there are any errors, retrace your steps. Did you miss something somewhere?

Don't be afraid to start over. The worst thing that can happen if you start over is that you have too many raw materials. Too many raw materials is not a problem. Too few is a problem. Try to figure out what is wrong, fix it, and don't hesitate to re-start this lab. Sometimes restarting is easier than trying to fix issues.

If there are no errors and everything looks okay, click the back arrow to return to the "Create Planned Order: Stock order" screen. If everything is okay, click the "Save" button.

SAP will give a small confirmation on the bottom left corner of the screen:

Planned order 379 will be created

Write this *Planned Order* # on line 1.5 of the *Relevant Information* form.

Switch back to your Stock/Requirements List.

Click "Refresh".

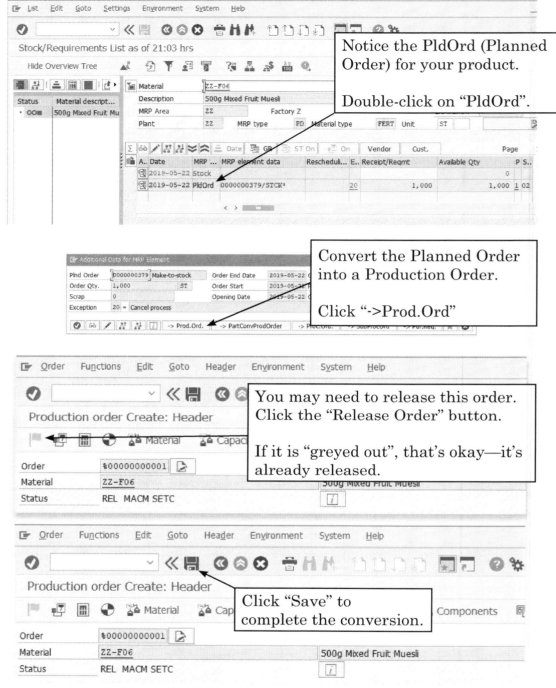

Notice the PldOrd (Planned Order) for your product.

Double-click on "PldOrd".

Convert the Planned Order into a Production Order.

Click "->Prod.Ord"

You may need to release this order. Click the "Release Order" button.

If it is "greyed out", that's okay—it's already released.

Click "Save" to complete the conversion.

You'll receive a message similar to this:

✔ Order number 1000219 saved

Write this *Prod. Order* # on line 1.6 of the *Relevant Information* form.

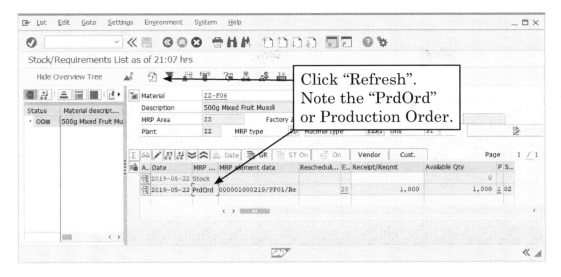

At this point, you've submitted two purchase orders (POs), received the necessary raw materials for 1,000 of your product, and created a Production Order to manufacture those products.

Within our SAP system, your finished products are being manufactured.

Confirming Your Production Order

Within the "real world", you would never create a production order and then immediately confirm it. Depending on the product, this could take several hours, several days, several weeks, several months... you get the idea. But, through the magic of academics, we'll pretend that this production order will be manufactured and completed within mere moments.

Switch back to your other session. Make sure you're back at the main SAP menu (or try /nco15!).

Transaction Code: Co15

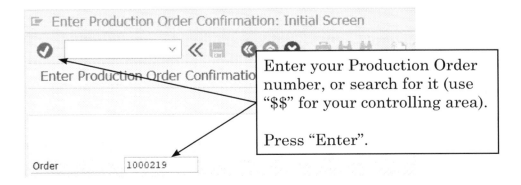

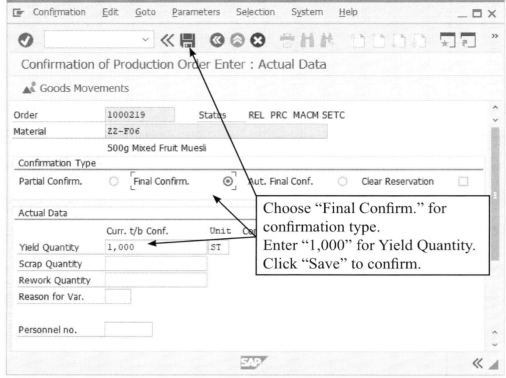

You should receive a message similar to this:

✅ Confirmation saved (Goods movements: 9, failed: 0)

If it says "Confirmation saved", but also includes failed movements, fear not.

Your product should be available. If you do not receive some form of the above message, re-trace your steps. Did you miss something along the way?

Confirm Stock of Your Finished Product

Close the "Enter Production Order Confirmation" session and switch to your other SAP session with the "Stock/Requirements List".

You should now have 1,000 of your 500 gram product produced and available for sale. This will show up under the "Available Qty" column header within the Stock/Requirements List.

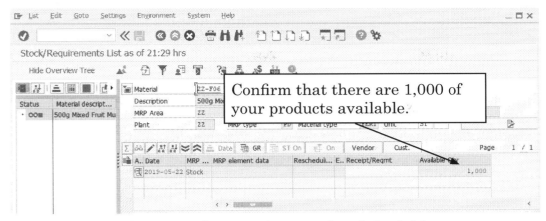

Confirm that there are 1,000 of your products available.

If you have 1,000 of your product, you've completed the lab!

If you are completing this lab as a graded assignment, use your print screen key, snipping tool, or other screen capture software to copy the Stock/Requirements list. Open MS Word and paste the screen shot into the word file.

Your screen shot MUST be legible.

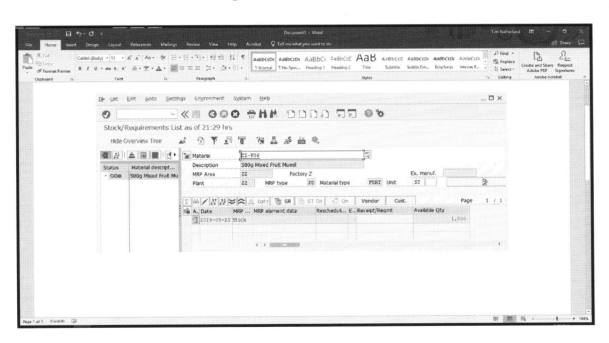

The above image shows a legible screen shot. The important details from the screen are available and legible within the standard Word Document size.

You may not receive credit for completing this lab if your screen shot is illegible.

An example of an illegible screen shot is on the next page.

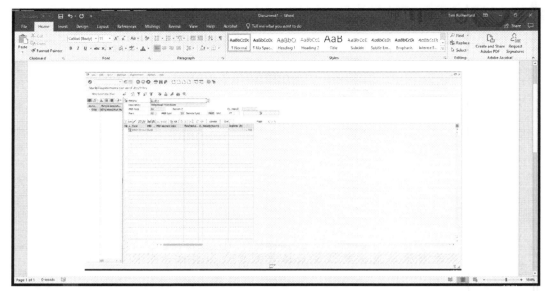

As you can see, it is nearly impossible to read this screen shot. Crop your screen shot so that the important details are legible.

Your instructor will let you know how to submit this document. Unless you have been instructed to print this document, do not submit anything but this MS Word document which includes your screen shot. No Excel files, no JPEG/PNG files, etc. Only MS Word documents.

Save the MS Word file as:

"Last_Name - $# - Lab 01" (i.e., "Rutherford – Z6 - Lab 01")

Make a note of where you are saving your file.

Unless you've been instructed otherwise, submit this Word file into your LMS (Learning Management Software such as D2L, Blackboard, Canvas, etc.) under the "Lab 01" assignment.

Feel free to close all open SAP windows and log off.

> **If you are using a computer lab: if you log off or are logged off for inactivity before uploading this file, you may lose the file.**

Lab 02 - Sales Order to Delivery

Selling Your Finished Goods

Within this lab you will sell 1,000 of your specific 500g muesli product.

> ****Important Steps *Before* You Start!****
> This lab presumes that you have already
>
> 1. Completed SAP Lab 01 manufacturing 1,000 of your product,
> 2. Changed your SAP GUI theme to "Blue Crystal", and,
> 3. Learned basic SAP GUI Navigation techniques.
>
> If you have not, complete the Pre-Labs: "Logging on to SAP" and "Navigating SAP", and, SAP Lab 01 before you start!
>
> **Instructors: Before your students begin these labs you must log on as "admin" and run ZSIM_START to prepare the client for the Extended Manufacturing Game. This must be repeated on the 1st of the month.

Log on using the same server / client / user ID / password from Lab 01.

Creating a Sales Order

Transaction Code: VA01

You'll be presented with the Create Sales Document screen:

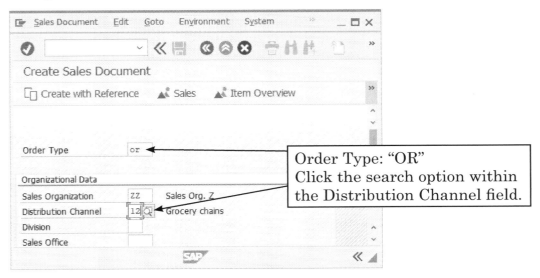

Order Type: "OR"
Click the search option within the Distribution Channel field.

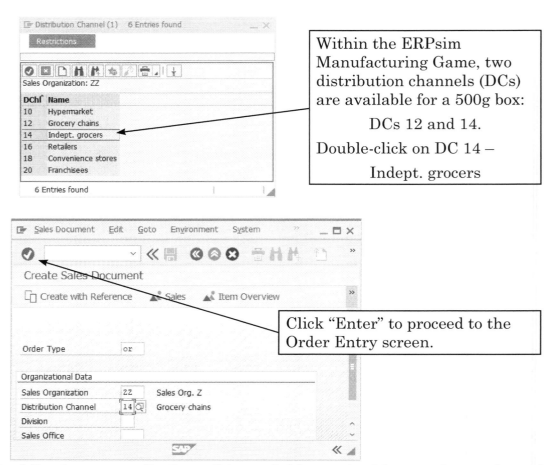

Within the ERPsim Manufacturing Game, two distribution channels (DCs) are available for a 500g box:

DCs 12 and 14.

Double-click on DC 14 – Indept. grocers

Click "Enter" to proceed to the Order Entry screen.

The following screen displays all input fields required for creating a sales order. As you'll see, the common database used within SAP comes in quite handy for the salesperson taking this order.

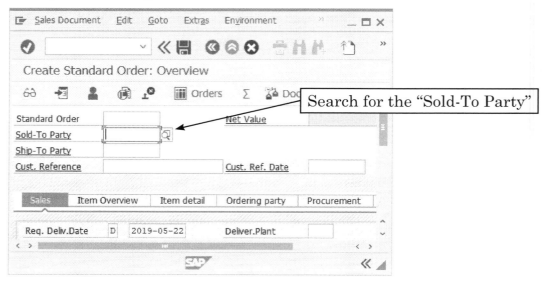

Search for the "Sold-To Party"

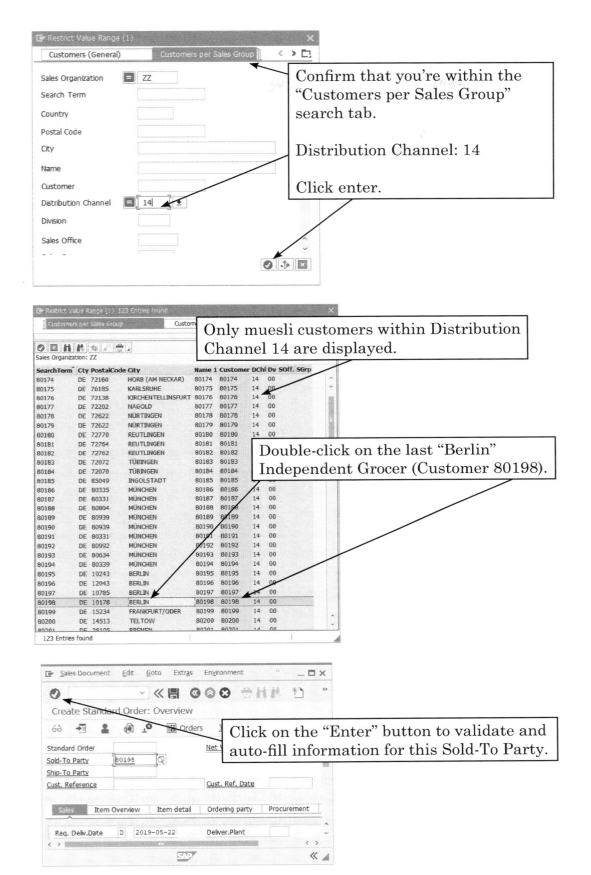

Confirm that you're within the "Customers per Sales Group" search tab.

Distribution Channel: 14

Click enter.

Only muesli customers within Distribution Channel 14 are displayed.

Double-click on the last "Berlin" Independent Grocer (Customer 80198).

Click on the "Enter" button to validate and auto-fill information for this Sold-To Party.

After clicking "Enter", you'll see that information is updated on the screen.

Pulling from the *common database*, SAP has automatically filled in the remaining information for the purchasing party, including payment terms.

Note that the dates are formatted: Year, Month, Day.

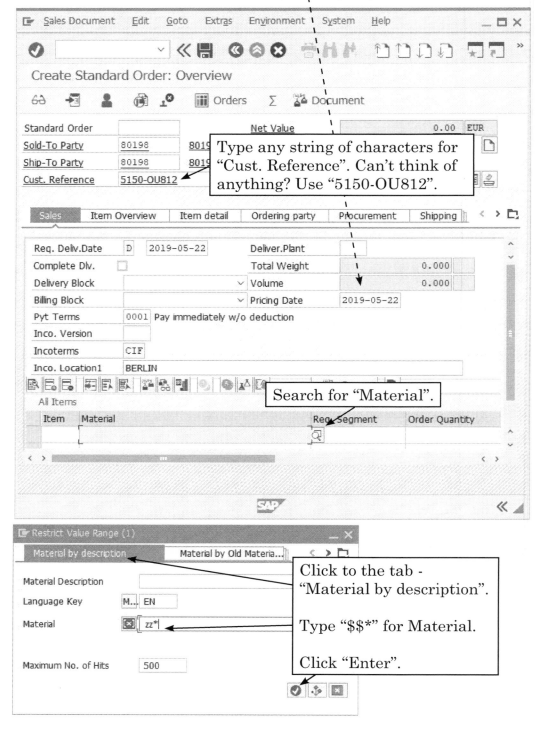

The result's long list of materials may be surprising to you. This list not only includes the Finished Products and Raw Materials for the Manufacturing Game, but also the various products available within all of the ERPsim games, including the Distribution Game and the Logistics game.

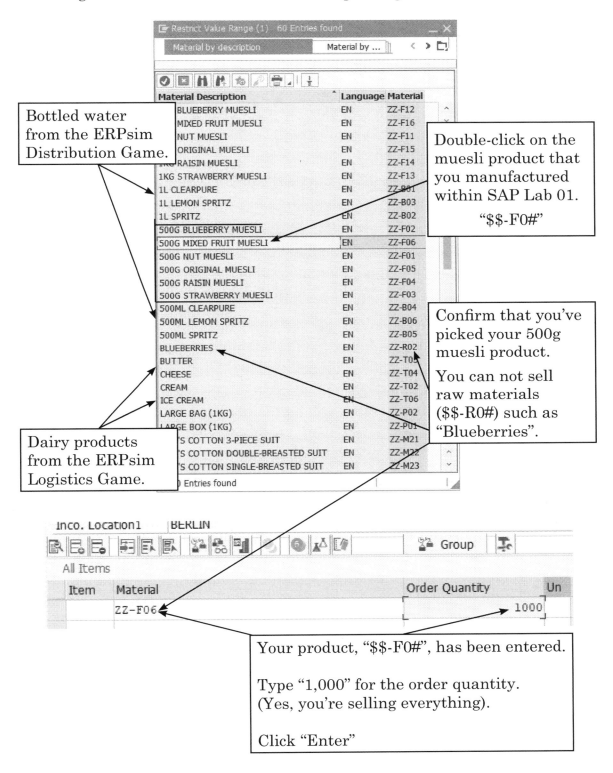

Bottled water from the ERPsim Distribution Game.

Double-click on the muesli product that you manufactured within SAP Lab 01.

"$$-F0#"

Confirm that you've picked your 500g muesli product.

You can not sell raw materials ($$-R0#) such as "Blueberries".

Dairy products from the ERPsim Logistics Game.

Your product, "$$-F0#", has been entered.

Type "1,000" for the order quantity.
(Yes, you're selling everything).

Click "Enter"

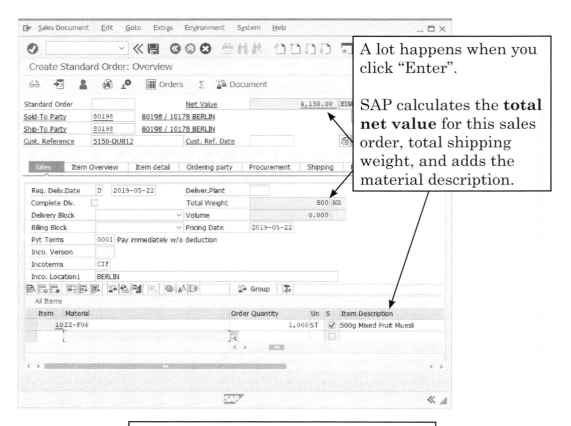

A lot happens when you click "Enter".

SAP calculates the **total net value** for this sales order, total shipping weight, and adds the material description.

Write this order's *Net Value* on line 2.1 of the *Relevant Information* form.

Even with the information pulled from the *common database*, SAP has not validated that this product is in stock. At this point, if you hadn't completed SAP Lab 01, you could get this far without an error. In fact, you could place this order without an error. SAP allows companies to place orders for products that aren't available as some manufacturers create the product after the order has been placed. These are "Made to Order" manufacturers. Within ERPsim, however, we are a "Make to Stock" manufacturer, which means that we create the stock and then sell it. There are no back-orders within ERPSim. If there is no stock, the order cannot be placed.

Before placing the sales order, let's see if there is enough available inventory to cover the sales order.

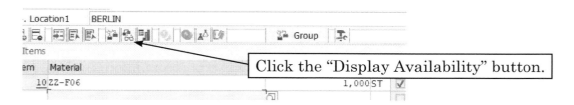

Click the "Display Availability" button.

Available to Promise

This checks for inventory availability based on *this exact sales order*.

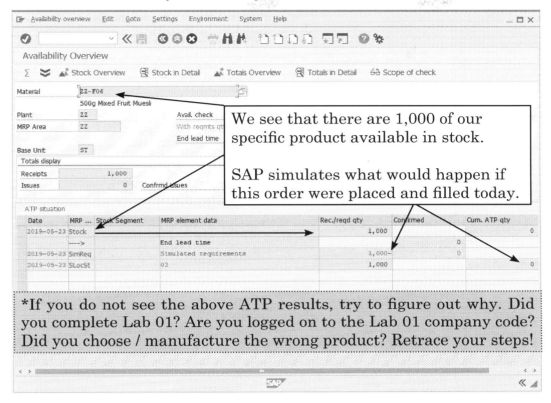

Within this screen, SAP simulates what would happen if the order were to be placed today, given that fulfillment states that it will ship today. This is important if there are multiple orders for the same product being placed at once. We don't just want to know how much is in stock, we want to know how much of that stock we can use for our order.

Provided you successfully completed SAP Lab 01, and you've typed everything correctly, you should see a similar screen confirming availability of your product. If you do not, re-trace your steps. What did you miss? Sometimes it's easier to re-start than to try and fix a mistake. Don't be afraid to start from scratch. If you never completed SAP Lab 01, complete it before starting this lab.

If you received no errors, click the "back" button to return to the order screen, click the "Save" icon to save this order.

You will receive a message like this:

> Write this *Standard Order* # on line 2.2 of the *Relevant Information* form.

Your order has now been submitted to the system, and has interacted with SAP in many areas.

> Remember that the benefit of an ERP system is the *common database*; all information is available across all functional areas to everyone who needs it. Let's look at one area that has responded to this change.

Go back to the SAP Menu.

Transaction Code: MD04

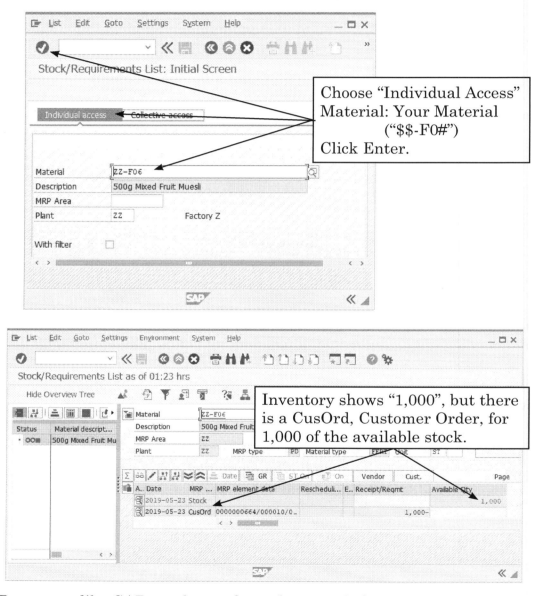

ERP systems like SAP can be configured to watch for these customer orders and alert the production manager to unexpected increases in product demand. It's important for inventory managers to do more than watch what is in stock. As we can see, there are 1,000 products available, 1,000 sitting "in stock", but all of them are being sold. A proactive production/inventory manager will work to replace this stock immediately.

This leads us to another issue—we have an order for our customer, but someone else could over-ride our order and allocate this stock to another customer. Let's allocate this to our customer before someone else orders it.

> ****Remember—it is unlikely that one person would be doing all of this. Typically, another department would take over the next few steps.**
>
> **For our academic purposes, you'll wear many hats.**

Create Outbound Delivery

Leave the "Stock/Requirements" window open and create a new session.

Transaction Code: VL01N

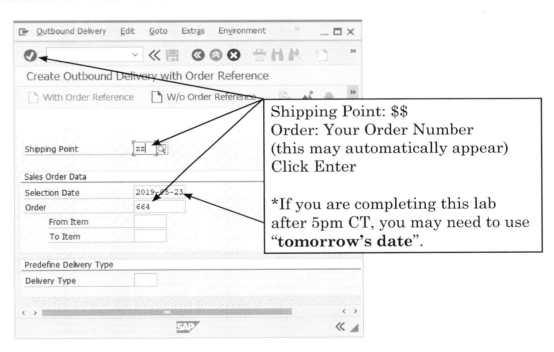

There is nothing else to do on this screen except to click "Save".

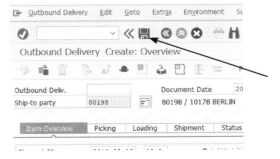

If you've been paying attention to detail, and you've seen no previous errors, you'll see a message like this:

✅ Outbound Delivery 80000663 has been saved

> Write this *Outbound Delivery* # on line
> 2.3 of the *Relevant Information* Form.

Switch to the "Stock/Requirements List" session. Click the "Refresh" button to see what this "Outbound Delivery" has done with inventory.

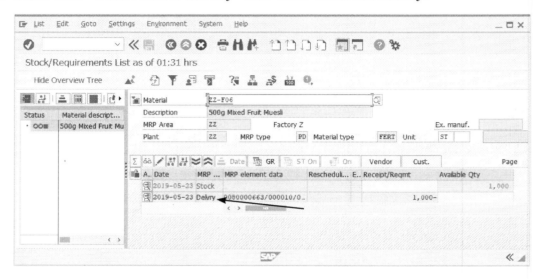

You're getting closer to claiming this inventory. It's now scheduled as a "Delivery". But, notice the stock—it's still at 1,000. Someone else could still claim this inventory. The next step goes to the warehouse where someone needs to "Pick, pack, and ship" the 1,000 boxes of Muesli.

Leave the "Stock/Requirements List" open and switch back to the other session.

Click "Back" until you've reached the SAP Menu.

Create Outbound Delivery – Picking your order

Transaction Code: VL02N

Your "Delivery order" may automatically appear. If not, type it or search for it. Click Enter to continue.

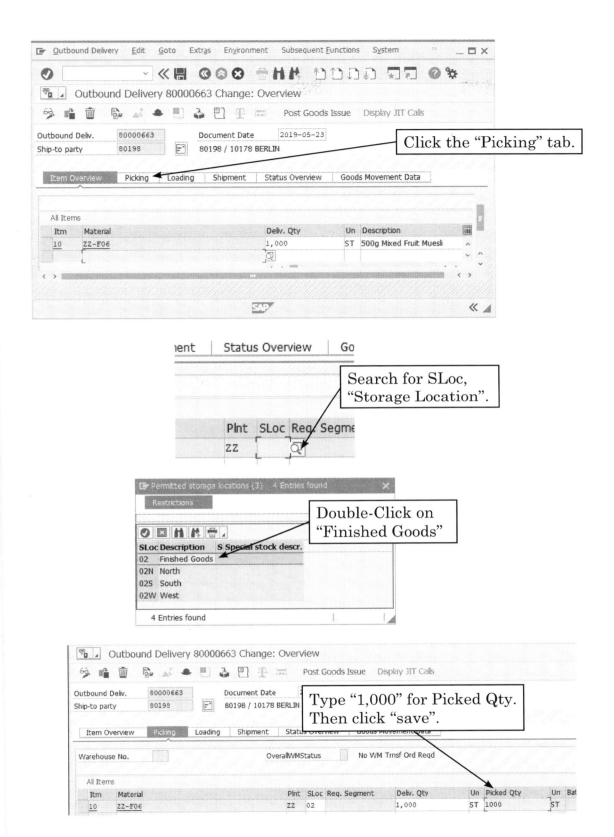

Click the "Picking" tab.

Search for SLoc, "Storage Location".

Double-Click on "Finished Goods"

Type "1,000" for Picked Qty. Then click "save".

You'll receive the message:

(This is the same "Outbound Delivery" you've been working with—no need to document it.)

Switch to the "Stock/Requirements List" session and click the Refresh button.

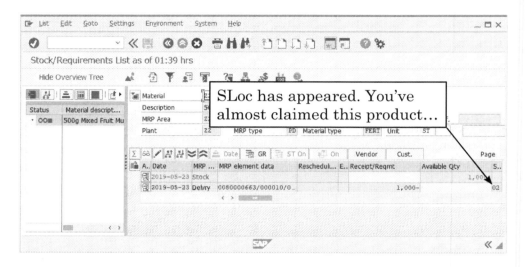

Leave the Stock/Requirements List open and switch back to your other session.

Post Goods Issue

Transaction Code: VL02N

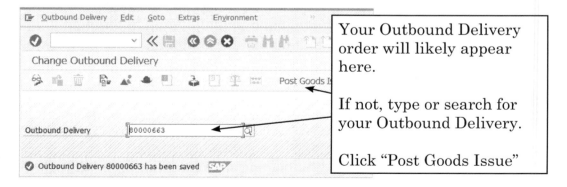

And, now it's officially your customer's product! Let's confirm.

Switch to the "Stock/Requirements List" and click Refresh.

What do you see?

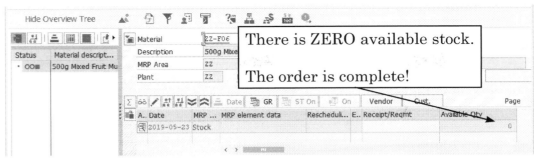

There is ZERO available stock.

The order is complete!

Document Flow

Switch back to the other session—you should still be at the "Change Outbound Delivery" screen.

(If you exited out of the transaction, open transaction code: VL02N)

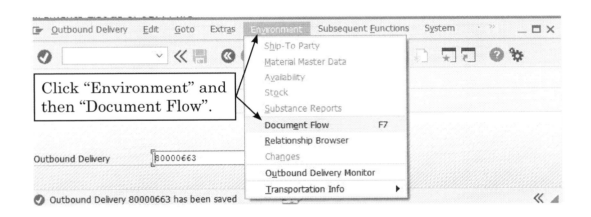

Click "Environment" and then "Document Flow".

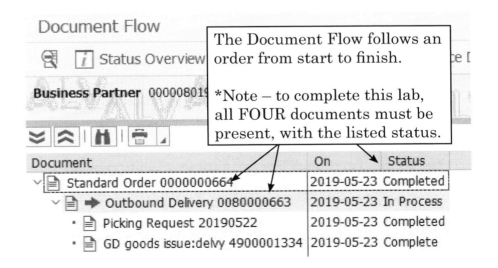

The Document Flow follows an order from start to finish.

*Note – to complete this lab, all FOUR documents must be present, with the listed status.

The Document Flow is great for trouble-shooting and tracing issues that may take place within the order entry and fulfillment process. A salesperson can check the order's status, someone in shipping can look back to see the original order. SAP gives each individual just enough information to do their portion of the process, but allows them full access to the details—as needed.

You have completed this lab! If you are submitting this lab as a graded assignment, take a screen shot of the Stock/Requirements list. Open MS Word and paste the screen shot into the word file.

Your screen shot MUST be legible. The following is not a legible screen shot.

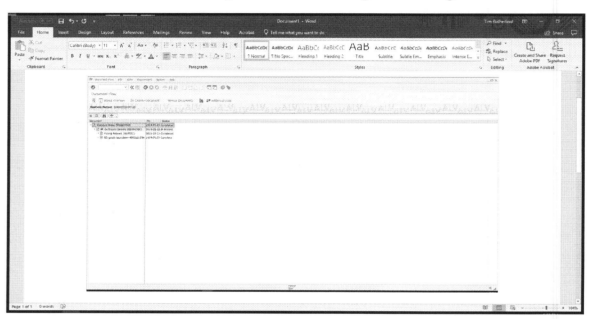

As you can see, it is nearly impossible to read this screen shot. Crop your screen shot down so that the important details are legible.

If your screen shot is not legible, you may not receive credit for completing this lab.

Save the MS Word file as:

"Last_Name - $# - Lab 02" (i.e., "Rutherford – Z6 - Lab 02")

Unless you've been instructed otherwise, submit this Word file into your LMS (Learning Management Software such as D2L, Blackboard, Canvas, etc.) under the "Lab 02" assignment.

Feel free to close all open SAP windows and log off.

Lab 03 – Accounting and Bookkeeping

No matter what you produce, or what you sell, you still have to account for the cash-flow within your company. Within this section we'll step through general accounting and cash-flow related bookkeeping, while watching ad-hoc financial statements.

> ****Important Steps *Before* You Start!****
> This lab presumes that you have already
>
> 1. Completed SAP Lab 02 selling 1,000 of your product,
>
> 2. Changed your SAP GUI theme to "Blue Crystal"
>
> If you have not, complete SAP Lab 02 before you start!
>
> ****Instructors:** Before your students begin these labs you must log on as "admin" and run ZSIM_START to prepare the client for the Extended Manufacturing Game. This must be repeated on the 1st of the month.

Let's take a look at the company's financials first.

Ad-hoc Financial Statements

Transaction Code: F.01

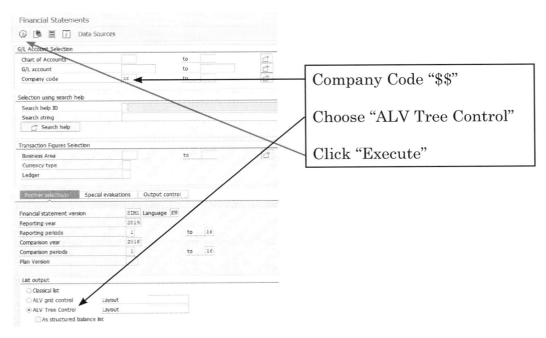

Company Code "$$"

Choose "ALV Tree Control"

Click "Execute"

You'll receive a warning, but don't pay attention to it. Click "Enter" to continue.

Remember that these financial statements reflect what you and your group have been doing within your company code; your numbers will vary. However, if you're all starting lab 03 at once, you should see one major item:

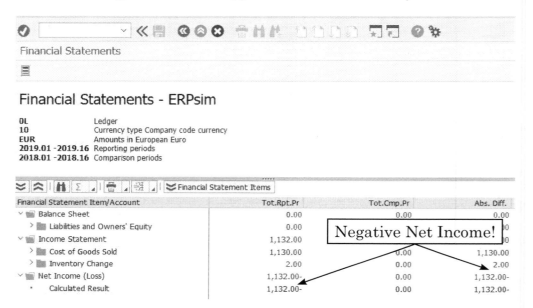

Why do you have negative net income? You've sold something, presumably at a profit. But even that sale isn't showing. Why?

Expand the following folders: Income Statement, Cost of Goods Sold:

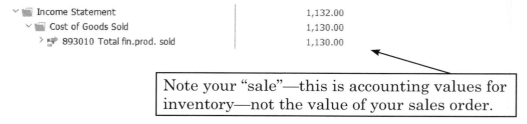

And why do you have negative net income?

Think back to what we accomplished within SAP Lab 02. We sold 1,000 products, we pick-pack-and-shipped. And wait… the sales order for 1,000 products had a larger total? Why isn't that on here? And… where's our cash? Shouldn't we have some cash from that order?

Did we forget something...? We never sent an invoice. And without an invoice, we can't receive payment from our customer.

Let's create the invoice. Leave this ad-hoc Financial Statement screen up. We'll come back to it throughout this lab. Create a new session.

Invoicing the Customer

Transaction Code: VF04

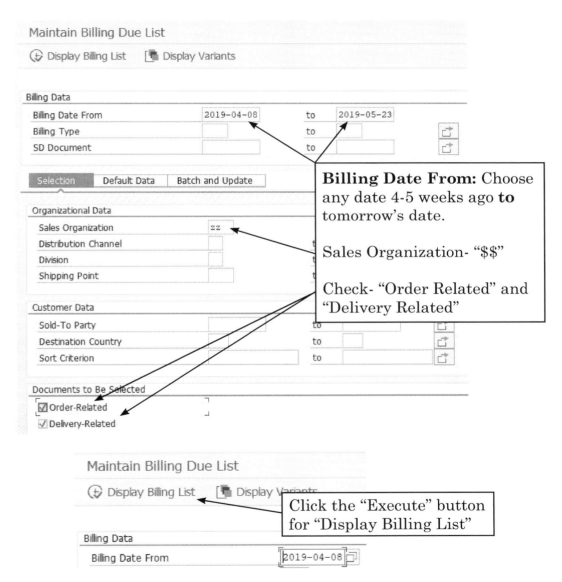

You may have more than one billing document here—remember that your group is also completing these labs and may be ahead of or behind you. If there is more than one billing document, use the document which corresponds with your "Outbound Delivery" number from SAP Lab 02. (Use the Relevant Information form at the end of this textbook.)

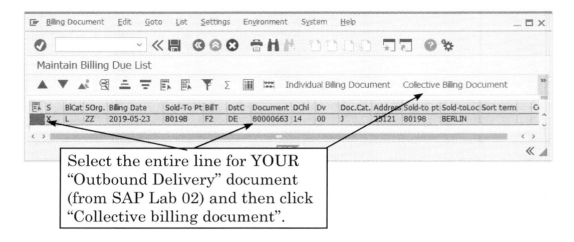

Select the entire line for YOUR "Outbound Delivery" document (from SAP Lab 02) and then click "Collective billing document".

It doesn't look like anything has happened, but an invoice has been created. And you need that invoice number to complete the next step.

Select the entire line for your "Outbound Delivery" document again. Under the heading "Environment", click "Display document."

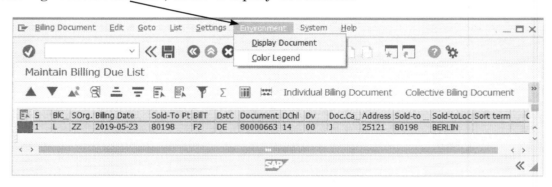

Your "Outbound Delivery" Document, from SAP Lab 02, will appear. Choose the header "Environment" and then click on "Document Flow".

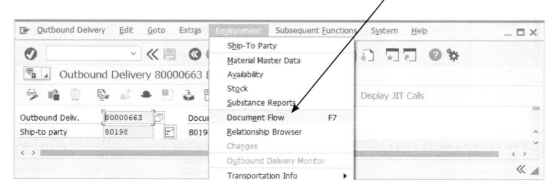

The next screen shows the updated "Document flow" since SAP Lab 02.

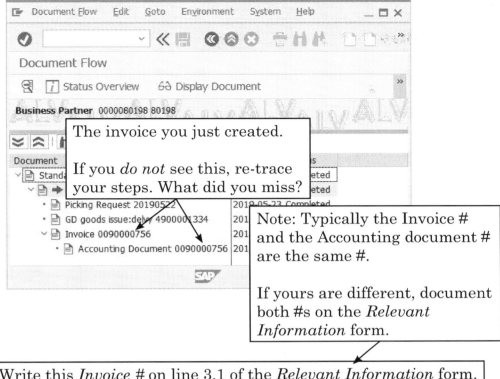

The invoice you just created.

If you *do not* see this, re-trace your steps. What did you miss?

Picking Request 20190522   2019-05-23 Completed
GD goods issue:deliv 490000334   201
Invoice 0090000756   201
   Accounting Document 0090000756   201

Note: Typically the Invoice # and the Accounting document # are the same #.

If yours are different, document both #s on the *Relevant Information* form.

Write this *Invoice* # on line 3.1 of the *Relevant Information* form.

In addition, we can see how this transaction has affected our company's financials. Switch over to your Financial Statements session (F.01).

There isn't a "refresh" button for this report, so you'll have to back out and go back in. Use the same parameters as last time. When you come back in, what do you see?

**Note: Remember that your numbers WILL be different. Your total sale and cost of raw materials are different—and the rest of your group is interacting within this same company. You should, however, see a difference when you return to this updated report.

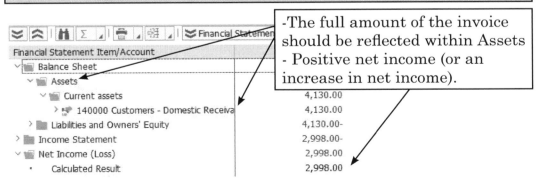

-The full amount of the invoice should be reflected within Assets
- Positive net income (or an increase in net income).

Financial Statement Item/Account	
Balance Sheet	
Assets	
Current assets	4,130.00
140000 Customers - Domestic Receiva	4,130.00
Liabilities and Owners' Equity	4,130.00-
Income Statement	2,998.00-
Net Income (Loss)	2,998.00
Calculated Result	2,998.00

But, wait—why did net income increase, but we've never received payment?

ERPsim runs accrual basis accounting, not cash basis accounting. All we need is a promise of payment and it counts as revenue. At the same time, note that we still haven't paid for our raw materials. With accrual basis accounting, cash is secondary to the documentation itself. An invoiced sales order counts as revenue. An invoice for raw materials counts as a liability.

Let's continue with every organization's dream—and receive payment for our sales order before we pay for the raw materials.

Switch back to your other session, and return to the main SAP menu.

Receive Payment from the Customer

Transaction Code: F-28

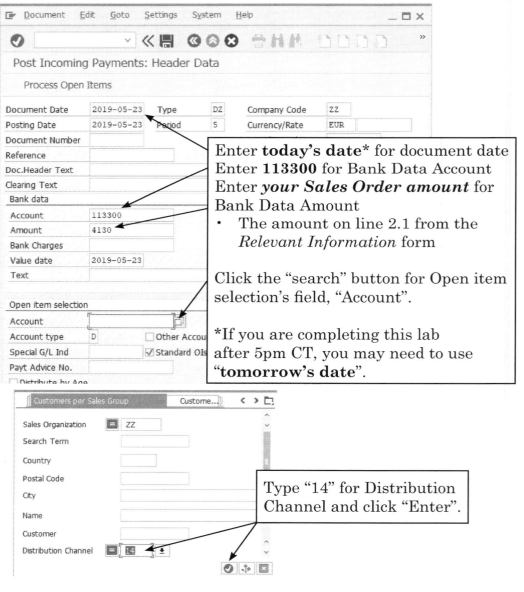

Do you remember who you sold to? The screen shots showed the last Distribution Channel 14 grocer in Berlin. Did you sell to them? If not, figure out who you sold to and choose them.

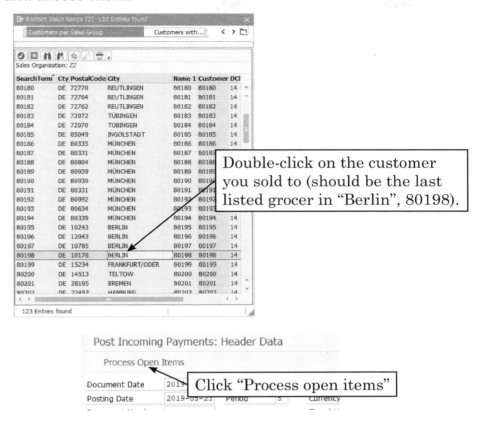

Double-click on the customer you sold to (should be the last listed grocer in "Berlin", 80198).

Post Incoming Payments: Header Data

Process Open Items

Click "Process open items"

Slow down as you move into the next screen.

This is bookkeeping. The person typically using these transactions will spend all day buzzing around between a few transactions. They are very familiar with the transactions and how to complete this process.

You are not the bookkeeper for this company. You are likely unfamiliar with these transactions. SAP assumes that you know what you're doing and will give limited feedback. This is not intuitive.

Remember to only work with your Accounting Invoice (Line 3.1 of the *Relevant Information* form) and your invoice amount (Line 2.1 of the *Relevant Information* form).

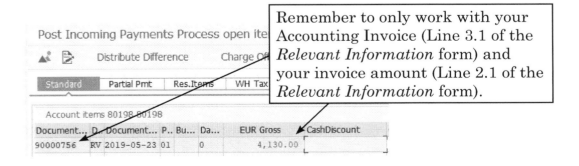

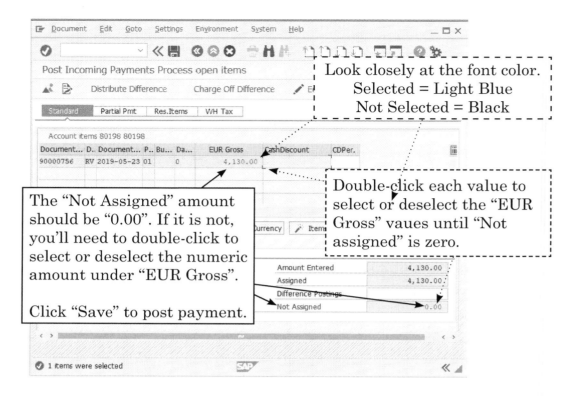

The "Not Assigned" amount should be "0.00". If it is not, you'll need to double-click to select or deselect the numeric amount under "EUR Gross".

Click "Save" to post payment.

Look closely at the font color.
Selected = Light Blue
Not Selected = Black

Double-click each value to select or deselect the "EUR Gross" vaues until "Not assigned" is zero.

Click back to the SAP menu—if you are given the message "Data will be lost", choose "Yes" to exit editing.

Now, switch to your Financial Statement session. Back out and go back in to refresh the data. What do you see? Anything different?

Your net income hasn't changed. Your total assets haven't changed. Even the balance for current assets hasn't changed. But you just received cash for your customer's invoice.

Open the "Current assets" folder to see what has happened.

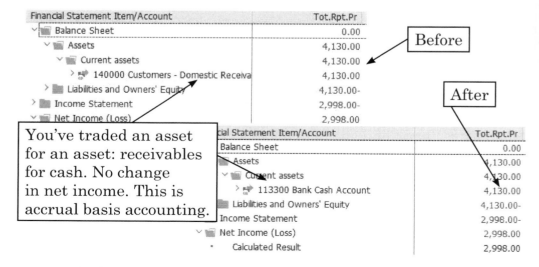

You've traded an asset for an asset: receivables for cash. No change in net income. This is accrual basis accounting.

Before

After

> Think about this—your cash account reflects your sales order's total value, but your net income is less. Why isn't your net income the same amount as your cash account?
>
> Remember, ERPsim uses accrual basis accounting. Your income statement updates as revenues and expenses are accrued. You may have cash in your account, but you still owe for those raw materials. Your net income already reflects the raw material expenses.

Switch back to the other session. You should already be at the SAP Menu. If not, click the back arrow until you've reached the SAP Menu.

Enter Incoming Invoice: Foodbroker Inc.

Transaction Code: MIRO

Remember that you purchased raw materials from two different organizations. One PO went to a food vendor, FOODBROKER INC. The other PO went to CONTINENTAL PRINTING. You'll have to receive and pay two different invoices.

Let's start with FOODBROKER INC.

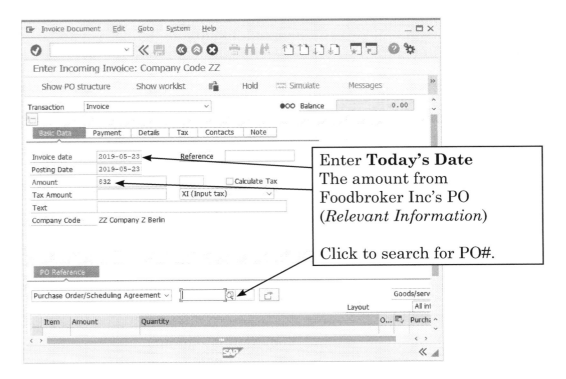

Enter **Today's Date**
The amount from Foodbroker Inc's PO (*Relevant Information*)

Click to search for PO#.

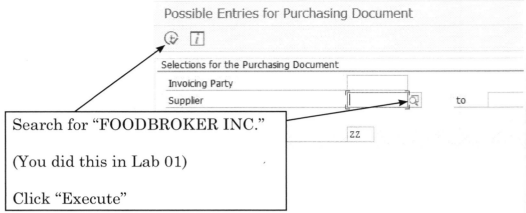

Possible Entries for Purchasing Document

Selections for the Purchasing Document

Invoicing Party

Supplier   to

ZZ

Search for "FOODBROKER INC."

(You did this in Lab 01)

Click "Execute"

Depending on where your group members are in this lab, you may see a list of available PO Numbers. Work ONLY with your PO Number, not your entire group's POs.

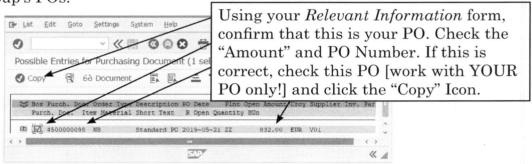

Using your *Relevant Information* form, confirm that this is your PO. Check the "Amount" and PO Number. If this is correct, check this PO [work with YOUR PO only!] and click the "Copy" Icon.

Click "enter" to populate the "Enter Incoming Invoice" screen with your PO details. Confirm that you are working with Foodbroker Inc. and that the values match what you expect. If everything looks okay, click on the simulate button (Simulate), which will bring up the following screen:

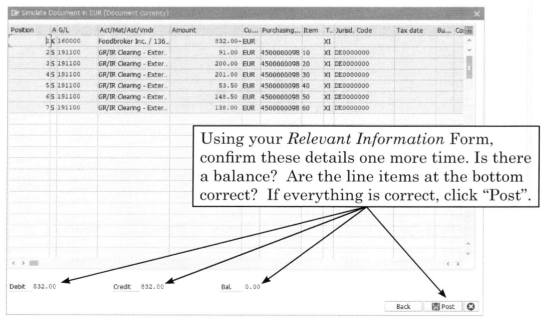

Using your *Relevant Information* Form, confirm these details one more time. Is there a balance? Are the line items at the bottom correct? If everything is correct, click "Post".

Received the error "Blocked for Payment"? Sometimes this error is an issue, other times it is not. It's also difficult to predict why you are receiving this error. Typically the error comes from an information mismatch between the "amount" entered, the selected vendor, or sometimes the date. If you are unable to post, something needs to be fixed. Back out and repeat this last step while carefully checking and confirming your information. If everything looks okay, click "post".

If you are able to post, it probably worked. Try the next step (Post Outgoing Payment). If you are unable to post payment for the invoice, re-visit this previous step. Do note that if you are able to complete the following step, the "blocked for payment" error was not an issue.

Click back to the SAP Menu.

Post Outgoing Payment

Transaction Code: F-53

This might sound wishy-washy, but we are using standard SAP accounting transactions. To preserve the integrity of our company's financial data, one little error can create unpredictable errors.

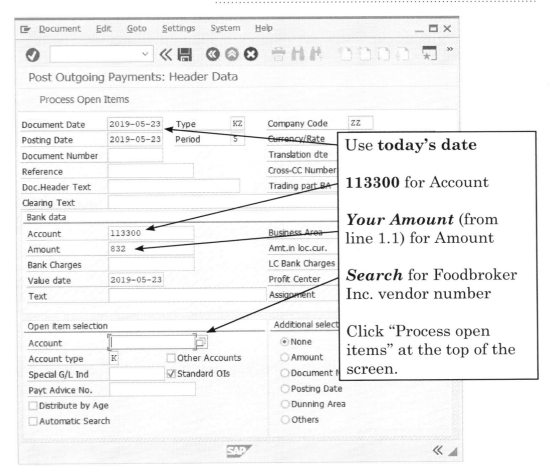

Use **today's date**

113300 for Account

Your Amount (from line 1.1) for Amount

Search for Foodbroker Inc. vendor number

Click "Process open items" at the top of the screen.

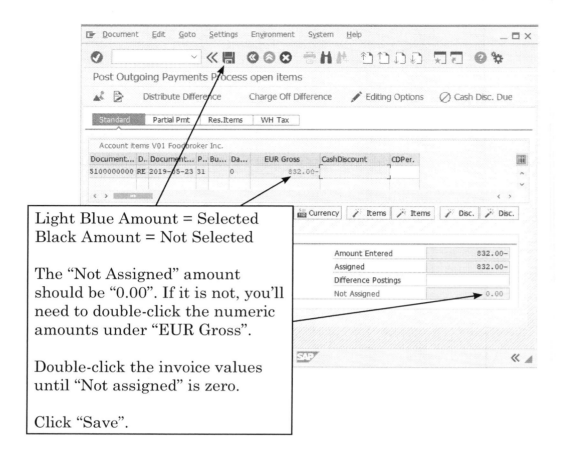

Light Blue Amount = Selected
Black Amount = Not Selected

The "Not Assigned" amount should be "0.00". If it is not, you'll need to double-click the numeric amounts under "EUR Gross".

Double-click the invoice values until "Not assigned" is zero.

Click "Save".

If you do not receive an error message, back out of this screen to reach the SAP Menu. Answer "Yes" to the following question:

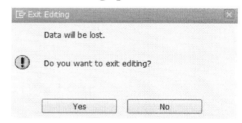

Now switch back to your Financial Statement session. Back out and go back in to refresh the data.

> Notice that, while your net income has stayed the same (depending on what your group members are doing, of course), the assets and liabilities have changed. This is accrual basis accounting.
>
> Net income changes as the expense is accrued. What we're doing now is taking care of the cash side of accounting.

Open the "Assets" and "Liabilities and Owners' Equity" folders to see what's listed under your current assets and current liabilities.

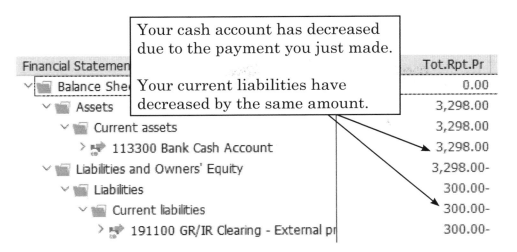

Financial Statement	Tot.Rpt.Pr
∨ 🗃 Balance She[...]	0.00
∨ 🗃 Assets	3,298.00
∨ 🗃 Current assets	3,298.00
> 🏷 113300 Bank Cash Account	3,298.00
∨ 🗃 Liabilities and Owners' Equity	3,298.00-
∨ 🗃 Liabilities	300.00-
∨ 🗃 Current liabilities	300.00-
> 🏷 191100 GR/IR Clearing - External pr	300.00-

Your cash account has decreased due to the payment you just made.

Your current liabilities have decreased by the same amount.

Now let's go back and finish up the remaining Current liabilities. You'll repeat the steps you just finished to complete the payment for Continental Printing.

> Remember that you purchased raw materials from two different organizations. One PO went to a food vendor, FOODBROKER INC. The other PO went to CONTINENTAL PRINTING. You'll have to receive and pay two different invoices.

Let's finish this section of our accounting lab by processing Continental Printing's invoice.

Switch back to your other session. Click the "Back" button until you've returned to the SAP Menu.

Enter Incoming Invoice: Continental Printing Co.

Transaction Code: MIRO

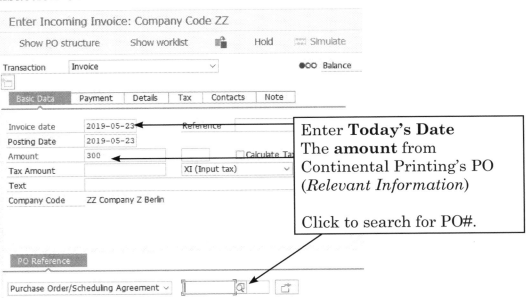

Enter **Today's Date**
The **amount** from Continental Printing's PO (*Relevant Information*)

Click to search for PO#.

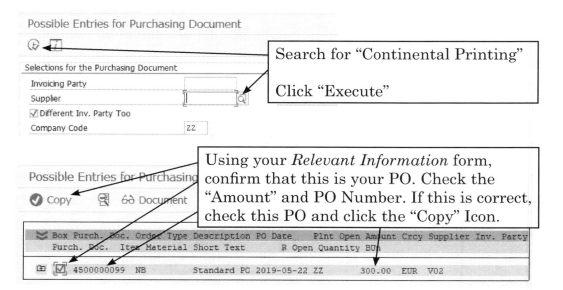

Search for "Continental Printing"

Click "Execute"

Using your *Relevant Information* form, confirm that this is your PO. Check the "Amount" and PO Number. If this is correct, check this PO and click the "Copy" Icon.

Click "enter" to populate the "Enter Incoming Invoice" screen with your PO details. Confirm that you are working with Continental Printing and that the values match what you expect. If everything looks okay, click on the simulate button (⁑ Simulate), which will bring up the following screen:

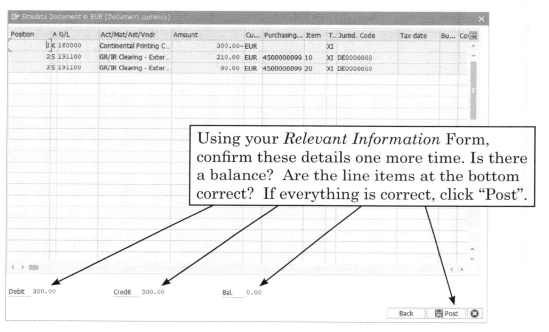

Using your *Relevant Information* Form, confirm these details one more time. Is there a balance? Are the line items at the bottom correct? If everything is correct, click "Post".

Received the error "Blocked for Payment"? Sometimes this error is an issue, other times it is not. If you are unable to post, something needs to be fixed. Repeat this last step carefully checking and confirming your information. If everything is entered correctly, click "post".

If you are able to post, it probably worked. Try the next step. If you are unable to post payment, re-visit this previous step. If you are able to post payment, the "blocked for payment" error was not an issue.

Click back to the SAP Menu.

Post Outgoing Payment

Transaction Code: F-53

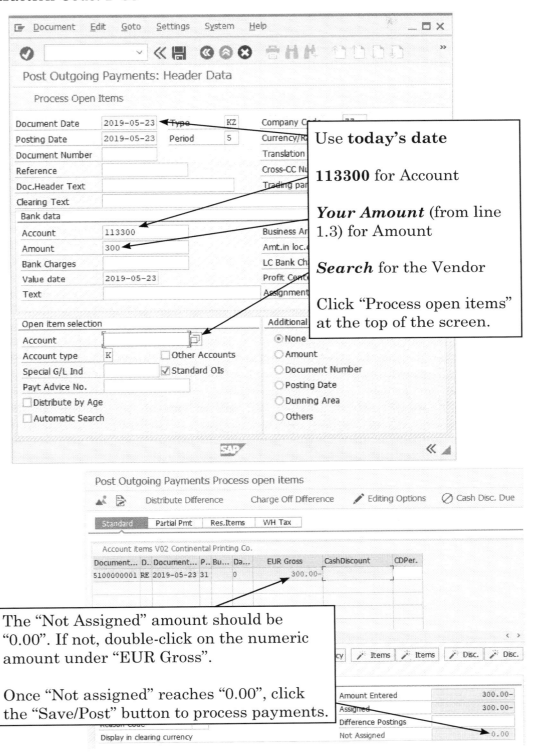

Use **today's date**

113300 for Account

Your Amount (from line 1.3) for Amount

Search for the Vendor

Click "Process open items" at the top of the screen.

The "Not Assigned" amount should be "0.00". If not, double-click on the numeric amount under "EUR Gross".

Once "Not assigned" reaches "0.00", click the "Save/Post" button to process payments.

Click back to the SAP Menu. Click yes to the following message:

Now switch back to your Financial Statement session. Back out and go back in to refresh the data.

Notice that, while your net income has stayed the same (depending on what your group members are doing, of course), the assets and liabilities have changed. Open the "current assets" and the "Liabilities and Owner's Equity" folder to see what's listed under your cash account and current liabilities.

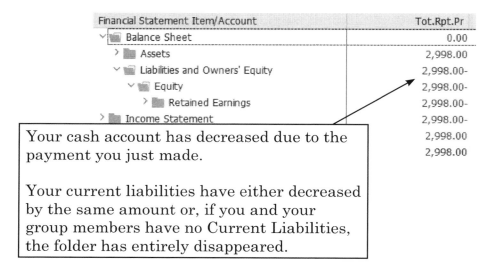

Invest in Your Company

The final transaction to complete will be to reinvest your available cash back into your company. There are two options for reinvestment within ERPsim.

One option is to decrease setup time between products. The default setup time is 8 hours, which means that every time you switch your production line from one product to another, you lose one third of one day's total production (8 of the available 24 hours). With the simulation running, If your group's strategy is to focus on one or two products, reduction of setup time may not make much difference. If you plan to switch between all twelve products, reducing your setup time may make a tremendous difference within your production efficiency.

The other option is to increase the capacity of your production line. The default capacity is 24,000 products per day. Remember that 24,000 per day is —after—

setup time between products. Depending on your strategy, increased capacity may make more of an impact on your production.

Or, any combination of the above two.

From the ERPsim Extended Manufacturing Game job aid, here are some milestones with their corresponding investment amounts:

PRODUCTION CAPACITY	
Capacity (units/day)	24,000
Additional Capacity (€ per 1,000 units)	1 000 000**

**Investing in additional capacity will increase equipment depreciation costs*

SETUP TIME	
Setup time (hours)	Investment (€)
8	–
7	50 000
6	125 000
5	250 000
4	500 000
3	1 250 000

The above euro amounts are just milestones. Any amount you invest will make a difference. For more details on the exact formulas for either investment, read through ERPsim's Manufacturing Game Participant's Guide and slides.

Within this lab, you'll invest cash to decrease your setup time. To start, determine your available cash—specifically based on your product's sales.

Turn to the Relevant Information form at the end of the textbook.

Take the total from your Sales Order (line 2.1) and subtract the total cost of your Raw Materials (line 1.1 + line 1.3). The remaining balance is your available cash.

$$2.1 - (1.1+1.3)$$

Sales Order – Total Raw Material Cost

= Available Cash for Reinvestment

Write this total down on line 3.2 on the Relevant Information form.

Switch from your Financial Statement session to the other session. Click the Back button until you reach the SAP Menu. Click through any messages asking you to save.

Setup Time Reduction

From the Job Aid:

Transaction Code: FB50

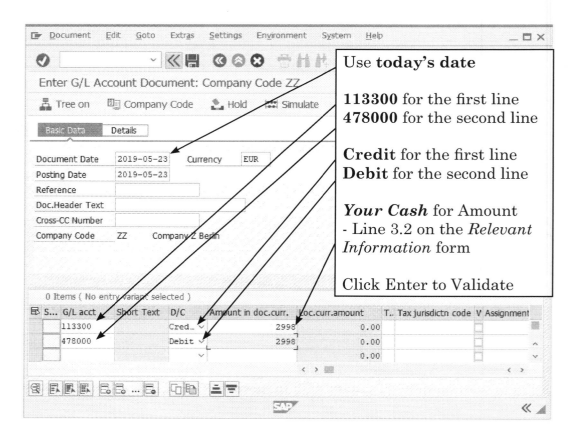

Upon validation (clicking Enter), the common database will be queried. Notice the accounts you're using here. 478000 is the G/L account for "Lean mfg expenses". You're, essentially, paying a consultant to help you streamline your production process with "lean manufacturing techniques".

2 Items (No entry variant selected)

S...	G/L acct	Short Text	D/C	Amount in doc.curr.	Loc.curr.amount
✓	113300	Bank Cash	Cred... ∨	2,998.00	2,998.00
✓	478000	Lean mfg ex.	Debit ∨	2,998.00	2,998.00

If there are no errors, click "Save" to post this transaction.

Switch back to your Financial Statement session, backing out and going back in to "refresh" the statement.

Quite a change! Your assets have dropped and your net income has also dropped. Depending on your group's progress, your net income could be minimal, zero, or negative!

> Why do you have a minimal balance for net income? Open the "Current assets" folder. You may see a negligible amount of "Raw materials". Remember back in Lab 01 when SAP rounded your raw material PO? These are those extra raw materials. Their value shows up as "equity" on the balance sheet, which is "Net Income" on the income statement.

Paying a consultant for "lean manufacturing" expertise is an instant expense. As soon as the transaction is saved, regardless of when the consultant is paid, the expense is applied to the financial statement. Your net income has dropped.

Expand the "Revenues", "Sales, General, and Administrative Expenses" folders, and now the "Production improvement expenses" folder.

Financial Statement Item/Account	Tot.Rpt.Pr
∨ Income Statement	0.00
∨ Revenues	4,130.00-
> 800000 Sales revenues - domestic	4,130.00-
> Cost of Goods Sold	1,130.00
> Inventory Change	2.00
∨ Sales, General, and Administrative Expenses	2,998.00
∨ Production improvement expenses	2,998.00
> 478000 Lean Manufacturing Program E	2,998.00
∨ Net Income (Loss)	0.00
· Calculated Result	0.00

Use your print screen key, snipping tool, or other screen capture software to copy the financial statement. Open MS Word and paste the screen shot into the word file.

Like the image above, your screen shot MUST be legible. Crop your screen shot down so that the important details are legible.

The following is not a legible screen shot.

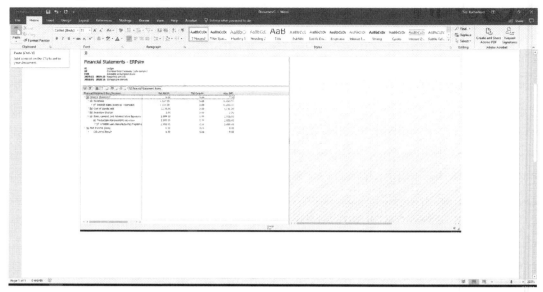

As you can see, it is nearly impossible to read this screen shot.

If your screen shot is not legible, you may not receive credit for completing this lab.

Do not submit anything but a MS Word document which includes your screen shot. No Excel files, no JPEG/PNG files, etc. Only MS Word documents.

Save the MS Word file as:

"Last_Name - $# - Lab 03" (i.e., "Rutherford – Z6 - Lab 03")

Submit this Word file into your LMS (Learning Management Software such as D2L, Blackboard, Canvas, etc.) under the "Lab 03" assignment.

Feel free to close all open SAP windows and log off.

Part II

The ERPsim Production Process

Section 03 - Sales Forecast

What is a Sales Forecast?

It's, quite simply, how much a company plans to sell within a given time period.

Every manufacturer requires a sales forecast. Period. This forecast is what puts everything into place; everything into motion. Without it, how does a company know how many of each product to manufacture? How do purchasing agents know which and how many raw materials to purchase? How do sales managers put together realistic sales quotas? How does a controller know if company goals are being met? The sales forecast is at the base of every manufacturing company's decisions. Operations, Supply Chain, Sales, Marketing... it all starts with the sales forecast.

Within the "real world", this is referred to as S&OP, or "Sales and Operations Planning". S&OP can be very complicated and often requires extensive research, statistical models, and many other factors. Within the ERPsim Manufacturing Game, the parameters are much simpler.

Within this section we'll calculate a starting forecast specific to the ERPsim Manufacturing Game.

The Reality of a Sales Forecast

Like with "real world" S&OP, if there were a guaranteed way to create an accurate sales forecast, every company would procure and/or manufacture exactly the number of products necessary to meet customer demand at any given time. In that reality tells us that this is impossible (companies are routinely overstock or out-of-stock), we have to accept that our sales forecast is a "guess". However, we do try to create as educated of a "guess" as possible.

Initial Sales Forecast: Creating an "Educated Guess"

While the next section details a calculation for your muesli company's initial forecast, it's merely an educated guess—a starting point. As you learn more about the simulation, your company, and determine a winning strategy, your initial forecast will undoubtedly change. And, as you'll find, even with ERPsim's simplicity, there will be no *perfect* sales forecast.

To start, you'll want to determine how many products you think you could (or should) sell within a day. Product sales are dependent on other factors (pricing, product, marketing, etc), but for production, you'll want to assume that you'll sell everything you manufacture within a day. Again, how to actually and consistently sell these products is another topic. Within this section, in creating our initial sales forecast, we'll presume to sell the same number of products as we manufacture within any given simulated day.

In order to calculate the number of products your company can manufacture within a day, you'll need to determine and understand your company's daily production capabilities and limitations—across a 20-day simulated round.

The ERPsim Manufacturing Game simulates a 24-hour day with possible production taking place across the full 24-hours. Without production upgrades, the initial production capacity is 1,000 products per hour, or 24,000 finished products across 24 hours/one day. This capacity continues at 24,000 per simulated day until another product is scheduled for production. Each time production shifts to a new product, there is mandatory set-up time. Without investment in set-up time reduction, the initial set-up time between products is 8 hours, or one third of one day's production (8 of the available 24 hours).

Without production improvements:

Daily Production Capacity: **24,000** Finished Goods (boxes of muesli—any size, any recipe)

Set-up time between products: **8** hours, or a third of one day's production

Depending on the length of the scheduled production run, your company's daily production capacity will end up somewhere between:

16,000 (1,000 * 16 hours) and 24,000 (1,000 * 24 hours)

Getting back to your daily sales—how many finished goods can you manufacture within a day? As a "guess", consider an average of the minimum and maximum production per day:

Minimum = 16,000   Maximum = 24,000

Average = **20,000** finished products per 24 hour day

Based on this average, you would presume to sell 20,000 finished goods per day. This is your average daily production.

But, let's take this a step further. Your company is capable of manufacturing twelve products. It is your goal to, at any given time, have all of the products you want to sell in stock and available for sale. With a good market price and reasonable marketing, you'll be spreading your average daily sales across all of those products.

How many of the twelve possible products should you produce at any time? That's part of your overall strategy. In general, it's best to limit the number of products you are manufacturing to match your production capabilities. Given the average of 20,000 finished products in one day and twelve products, producing all 12 products and keeping all of them in stock could prove to be quite a challenge.

To keep things simple, plan smaller and adjust the number of products as you learn more about the market.

In creating your initial forecast, plan for producing six of the available twelve products. Any six, any combination of 500 gram and 1 kilogram muesli.

Take the average daily sales and divide it among the 6 products:

20,000 (total products sold) / 6 (total products) =
3,334 (individual finished goods sold per day)

For Product One, you presume to sell 3,334 each day. Product Two, 3,334. Product Three, etc. etc.

However, your product requires raw materials and those raw materials must be ordered from a vendor. Within the ERPsim Manufacturing Game, lead-time for receiving delivery of raw materials is 1-5 days. Once the materials are in-stock, with 6 products and an average of 20,000 products manufactured per day, it may be 6 days before a product is even manufactured (manufacturing one product per day, six products, six days).

How many days between ordering raw materials and production of the sixth product?

Lead-time = 1-5 days   Production = 1-6 days

5 (max lead-time) + 6 (max production [total products])

Maximum Days to Product availability = (5 + 6) = 11

Simulated Day:	1-5	6	7	8	9	10	11
Daily Action:	Raw Material Lead Time	Product One	Product Two	Product Three	Product Four	Product Five	Product Six

The initial "educated guess" sales forecast within the ERPsim Extended

Manufacturing Game is:

11 (max. days to produce) * 3,334 (expected per-product sales per day) = 36,674

Recapping the calculation:

Daily production capacity is 24,000 with setup time between products of 8 hours or 1/3 of daily production (8 of the 24 available hours). The minimum production per day is 16,000 and maximum is 24,000. Your average daily production is 20,000.

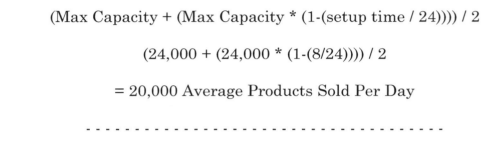

(Max Capacity + (Max Capacity * (1-(setup time / 24)))) / 2

(24,000 + (24,000 * (1-(8/24)))) / 2

= 20,000 Average Products Sold Per Day

- -

(Average Products Sold Per Day) / (Total Products to Manufacture)

(20,000 / 6)

= 3,334 (Individual Finished Goods Sold Per Day)

- -

Finished Goods Sold Per Day * (Max Lead Time + Total Products)
3,334 * (5 + 6)

= 36,674 Starting per Product Sales Forecast

Is 36,674 your actual forecast?

Within ERPsim, food raw material order quantities are rounded up to the nearest 10kg, while the packaging raw material order quantities and sales forecasts are rounded up to the nearest 1,000.

A sales forecast of 36,674 will be rounded up to the nearest 1,000, 37,000. When you actually execute MRP, both production and procurement will use 37,000 as the order quantity.

Like a sales forecast within the "real world", there are no guarantees that this is what you will sell. It is an educated guess based on the production limitations and a "best case" sales scenario.

It will, undoubtedly, need to be adjusted as you acquire additional information.

Why Would You Change Your Sales Forecast?

The only reason you would change your forecast is because your "educated guess" has become "better educated". You had to start somewhere. But, if you forecast for too much, you may have production bogged down on a product that isn't selling while you've run out of a product that is selling. Or, the opposite, if you forecast for too few of a product—below customer demand—you may find yourself constantly out-of-stock of the product. Both of these result in not having products available for sale, or a stock out. If you have frequent stock outs, you're losing revenue, and it is unlikely that you will be profitable.

Examples of why you'd change your forecast:

- Perhaps you've found that no matter what you do, you just can't sell one or two products. Maybe you'll choose to limit production of those products? Or, perhaps you'll stop producing them all-together.

- Perhaps you've found that you can't keep certain products on your shelves—and you're selling them at a profitable margin. If this is the case, you may choose to focus your production on those products and increase those products' forecast.

- You've increased your production capacity, or decreased set-up time, or reduced/increased the number of products you're manufacturing.

- Any combination of the above, or something else entirely. This is, after all, just a series of guesses. Hopefully educated guesses.

As you gain more experience within the ERPsim Manufacturing Game, you will find that your per-product forecast will vary. In addition, each ERPsim game is complete with a whole new market—with varying product preferences. It is unlikely that you'll keep the same forecast for all 12 products throughout each game, or from game-to-game.

Don't Change Your Forecast Too Often, or Too Quickly!

You'll want to gauge the market over a period of time. Remember that you're making "educated" guesses, and those guesses become more accurate with more information. Making quick decisions from day-to-day may leave you with inaccurate information—how do you know for sure that what you saw during one or a few days isn't the result of another team's poor playing?

Remember that you're competing with other teams selling the same products, within the same market. One team may manufacture 100,000 of a particular product, set their price below everyone else, and then sell out within 2-3 days. They have the same limitations as you—they can only produce about 24,000 per day. They are also limited by 6-11 days' worth of manufacturing lead-time. If they sell all 100,000 of their products within 2-3 days, they may steal market share for a few days, but then they will have a stock-out leaving your product as the only product available for sale. You notice a drop in sales and then your sales go back up to normal.

The following graph shows the total sales for one product across 7 competing teams.

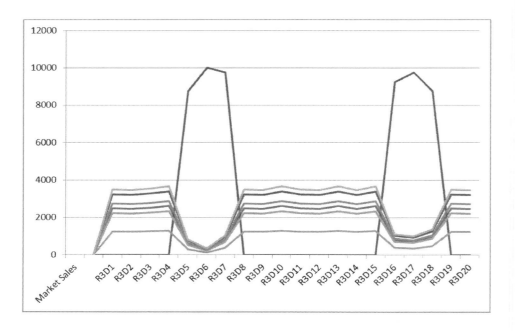

> Why did your sales drop? When should you make a decision?

As you can see, 6 of the teams show steady sales of this product, while one company shows completely erratic and inconsistent sales, oscillating between selling nothing and out-selling every other team.

As one of the 6 teams with steady sales, you have no idea what is happening with that 7th team. All you see is your team's sales—steady, steady, DROP, steady, steady, steady, DROP, steady.

If you make quick decisions regarding your sales, you may miss what's really going on.

Within the next graph, on Round 3, Day 6 (R3D6) sales have dropped dramatically. What do you do? Drop your price? Increase marketing? Or, wait and see what's really going on? Perhaps, as you can see with this overall market report, one team doesn't know what they're doing and are out-selling everyone for a limited time. If you make a quick decision, what happens next?

The following graph illustrates what may happen with a quick reaction:

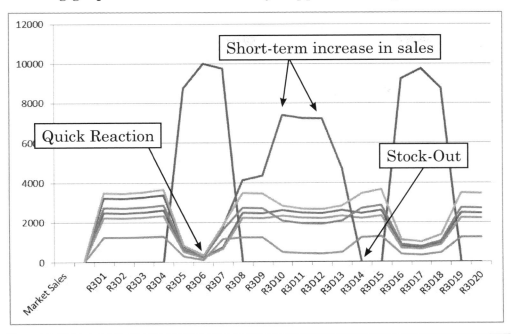

A quick reaction may boost sales in the short-term, but ends in a stock-out.

As you can see, the inexperienced team has created a great deal of product, priced it too low, and out-sold the market (which creates a drop in sales for all other teams). One of the seven teams makes a knee-jerk decision to lower their price, which results in a dramatic increase in sales, followed by a stock-out—they were unprepared for an increase in sales. A stock-out **rarely** leads to an increase in profits.

For the most part, making quick decisions may not help the longevity and long term profitability of your company. If something is working—and abruptly stops working—there may be other factors involved.

Educated Guess

Just remember that your initial sales forecast is always going to be a guess. However, there are ways to make your guess as educated as possible. Within the "real world", you'll want to research the market and make an educated guess. Within the ERPsim Manufacturing Game, you can start with an educated guess based on your capacity, set-up time, and lead-time. This forecast will need to be updated as the simulation continues, you gain additional information (through the provided reports), or you make changes to your infrastructure.

Creating a Sales Forecast in ERPsim's Manufacturing Game
Note—*Next Month*

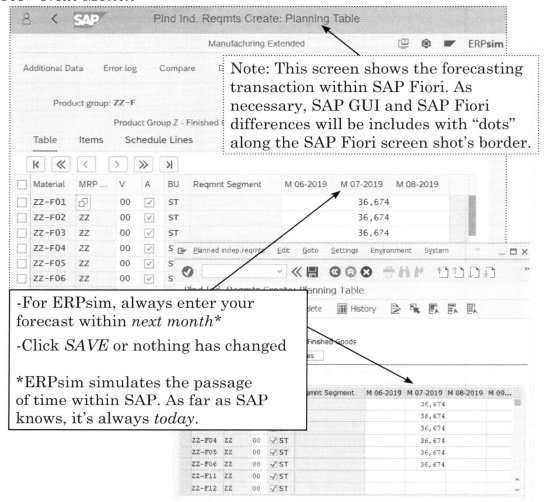

Note: This screen shows the forecasting transaction within SAP Fiori. As necessary, SAP GUI and SAP Fiori differences will be includes with "dots" along the SAP Fiori screen shot's border.

-For ERPsim, always enter your forecast within *next month**

-Click *SAVE* or nothing has changed

*ERPsim simulates the passage of time within SAP. As far as SAP knows, it's always *today*.

ERPsim's simulation software is "spoofing" the system. To the actual SAP servers, the date is always today. Your forecast needs to be in "next month" which is the next calendar month relative to *today's date*. Whether it's the first day of the actual month or the last day of the actual month, next month is always the next calendar month. Remember, the simulation is simulating the passage of time. The simulated day and round is not relevant to today's actual date, next month is always "next month".

Goal of a Sales Forecast within ERPsim

Within ERPsim, your goal is to sell *about* what you can produce within a day. If you're producing *about* what you sell within a day—at a profitable price—you're likely to increase your company's valuation.

How does a forecast fit into production? The next step is MRP.

Section 04 - MRP

What is MRP?

MRP is "Material Requirements Planning". MRP is complicated, a lot happens when you run MRP, but it is nothing more than planning. You can run MRP over and over, but all you do is create plans. Nothing is ordered nor produced.

What does MRP *plan?*

MRP plans for production. MRP looks at your sales forecast, looks at the raw material and finished goods inventory, the goods in production, and then calculates a *plan* to manufacture enough products to meet your sales forecast.

Within the ERPsim Manufacturing Game, running MRP creates two different plans: *planned purchase orders* and *planned production orders.*

Planned Purchase Orders

Purchase Orders (POs) are the official documents organizations utilize to authorize the order of raw materials, supplies, services, and anything else required from outside of the organization. These purchase orders document how much was purchased, which department authorized the purchase, which cost center is responsible for the expense, and anything else the organization might require to accompany the purchase of –anything– from outside of the organization.

Most organizations call *planned* purchase orders *Purchase Requisitions.* Purchase Requisitions are unauthorized, planned, or suggested *Purchase Orders.* Creating purchase requisitions is nothing but planning.

Within ERPsim's Manufacturing Game, running MRP creates the procurement *plan,* or *Purchase Requisitions,* to purchase the raw materials required for manufacturing muesli. Within ERPsim, just like in the "real world", planned purchase orders, or purchase requisitions, must be converted into *Purchase Orders* to officially authorize and order the raw materials.

Planned Production Orders

Production Orders instruct a manufacturing company on which products to produce, and how many of those products to manufacture.

Instead of manually creating production orders for each product, using ERPsim's MRP process, *planned production orders* are automatically created. Nothing is scheduled to be produced—this is the product *plan* based on the sales forecast and current inventory and production levels.

Once raw materials have been delivered, these planned orders can be converted into actual *Production Orders*. Nothing is manufactured and nothing is produced until these planned orders are converted into *Production Orders*.

Remember this about MRP:

MRP within SAP/ERPsim is planning. Nothing happens when you run MRP—except a plan is generated.

If you run MRP multiple times, MRP removes the active or current "plan" and creates a new "plan" based on the updated inventories and forecasts.

"Open" Purchase Requisitions (those that haven't been converted to Purchase Orders) are "closed" and then replaced by new "open" Purchase Requisitions. Planned Production Orders which have not been converted to Production Orders are also closed and replaced by new Planned Production Orders.

MRP creates plans based on the current inventories and forecasts.

How does MRP Know What to plan?

Before MRP is run, SAP needs to know the sales forecast for each product and the required raw materials within each manufactured product. This information is set within the Bill of Materials, or BOM.

Within SAP, you can see the BOM for any of the finished products.

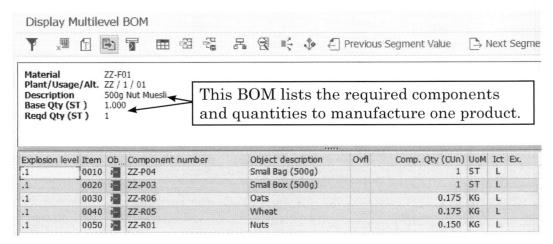

This BOM lists the required components and quantities to manufacture one product.

The BOM above lists the materials required for one 500g box of nut muesli cereal. For the 500g muesli products, the total food materials must equal 500g in weight: for nut muesli, 0.175kg Wheat, 0.175kg Oats, and 0.15kg of Nuts = .5kg or 500g. In addition, you'll see that the 500g product requires one small box and one small bag. The 1kg products require a total food material weight of 1kg as well as one large box and one large bag.

> **ERPsim Specific**—Within ERPsim, the time-frame for the sales forecast is from MRP run to MRP run, not round to round nor day to day. ERPsim is spoofing the system into seeing the passage of time, but within SAP, it's always today. While the sales forecast is entered into "next month", ERPsim uses that quantity each time MRP is run.
>
> Don't mistake the sales forecast for "total sales within a round". It is total sales from MRP run to MRP run.

Running MRP

We have our sales forecast (from the previous section), we have the BOM. Now what?

Within SAP, and specifically within the ERPsim Manufacturing Game, you execute one SAP transaction and MRP has been run. The transaction is simple, but a lot happens when you run this transaction.

Moving forward from the Sales Forecast section we'll walk through the MRP process for the very first time you run MRP within the ERPsim Manufacturing Game. We'll start with our initial calculated sales forecast of 36,674 and specifically track $$-F01, 500g Nut Muesli.

> Remember that ERPsim is programmed to round your forecast up to the nearest 1,000. This means that a forecast of 36,674 will be rounded up to 37,000. While you can look at your forecast in MD61 and it will show 36,674, procurement and production will use the rounded forecast: 37,000.
>
> From this point forward, the forecast will be referred to as 37,000 even though the calculated forecast, and the saved forecast, is 36,674.

The MRP Process – How is it Calculated?

Using the BOM for 500g Nut Muesli, MRP calculates the number of raw materials necessary to meet your sales forecast. MRP looks at your sales forecast and then compares it to your current inventory/stock levels for that finished product. At the start of the simulation your inventory is ZERO for all finished goods. You also have nothing scheduled for production, so the production numbers do not factor into the calculation.

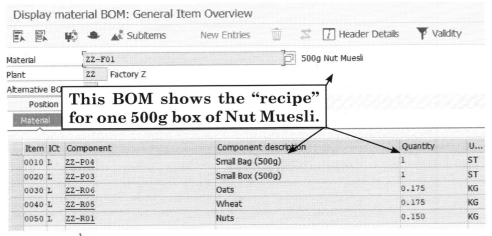

Inventory Report: Round 1 Day 01

SLoc	Material	Material description	Stock	Reserved	Unit
02	ZZ-F01	500g Nut Muesli	0	0	ST
	ZZ-F02	500g Blueberry Muesli	0	0	ST
	ZZ-F03	500g Strawberry Muesli	0		
	ZZ-F04	500g Raisin Muesli	0		
	ZZ-F05	500g Original Muesli	0	0	ST
	ZZ-F06	500g Mixed Fruit Muesli	0	0	ST

Zero finished product in stock

Using 37,000 as the forecast, MRP calculates that all 37,000 of the sales forecast must be manufactured for this finished product.

From here, MRP looks at your current raw material inventory for current stock levels. MRP will calculate and *plan* to order only enough raw materials to create 37,000 500g Nut Muesli.

The BOM tells MRP which raw materials are required for this finished product:

Display material BOM: General Item Overview

Subitems   New Entries   Header Details   Validity

| Material | ZZ-F01 | 500g Nut Muesli |
| Plant | ZZ | Factory Z |

This BOM shows the "recipe" for one 500g box of Nut Muesli.

Item	ICt	Component	Component description	Quantity	U...
0010	L	ZZ-P04	Small Bag (500g)	1	ST
0020	L	ZZ-P03	Small Box (500g)	1	ST
0030	L	ZZ-R06	Oats	0.175	KG
0040	L	ZZ-R05	Wheat	0.175	KG
0050	L	ZZ-R01	Nuts	0.150	KG

For each of the listed raw materials, MRP will then calculate the quantity of each raw material to purchase. In order to do this, MRP looks at the current raw material inventory:

88	ZZ-P01	Large Box (1kg)	0	0	ST
	ZZ-P02	Large Bag (1kg)	0	0	ST
	ZZ-P03	Small Box (500g)	0	0	ST
	ZZ-P04	Small Bag (500g)	0	0	ST
	ZZ-R01	Nuts	0	0	KG
	ZZ-R02	Blueberries	0	0	KG
	ZZ-R03	Strawberries	0	0	KG
	ZZ-R04	Raisins	0	0	KG
	ZZ-R05	Wheat	0	0	KG
	ZZ-R06	Oats	0	0	KG

Because the simulation has just started, there is no raw material inventory in stock. MRP must calculate for the purchase of all required raw materials to match the initial sales forecast.

Once the calculations are complete, MRP creates a *purchase requisition,* a planned purchase order, for each of the raw materials:

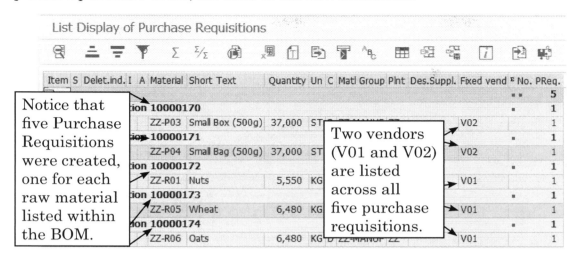

Notice that five Purchase Requisitions were created, one for each raw material listed within the BOM.

Two vendors (V01 and V02) are listed across all five purchase requisitions.

Within the above purchase requisitions, you can see the quantity for each raw material. Why does it list 37,000 boxes and bags, but far fewer of the other three raw materials?

Material	Short Text	Quantity	Un
10000170			
ZZ-P03	Small Box (500g)	37,000	ST
10000171			
ZZ-P04	Small Bag (500g)	37,000	ST
10000172			
ZZ-R01	Nuts	5,550	KG
10000173			
ZZ-R05	Wheat	6,480	KG
10000174			
ZZ-R06	Oats	6,480	KG

Look back at the BOM on the previous page. Note that each finished product requires one box and one bag, but the food raw materials are a portion of the total 500g per finished product. Food raw material purchases are made in quantities of 1kg for each material. While your forecast is for 37,000 finished products, you only need to order the portion of each food raw materials to complete 37,000 finished 500g products. For 500g Nut Muesli:

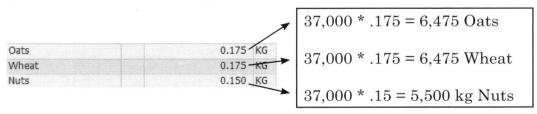

Oats		0.175	KG
Wheat		0.175	KG
Nuts		0.150	KG

$37,000 * .175 = 6,475$ Oats

$37,000 * .175 = 6,475$ Wheat

$37,000 * .15 = 5,500$ kg Nuts

Remember rounding... $37,000 * .175 = 6,475$. MRP, without explanation, has rounded 6,475 *up* to 6,480 within the Purchase Requisition.

In addition to planning the purchase of raw materials, MRP also creates a *planned production order*.

To see your *planned production order*, visit the Stock Requirements List:

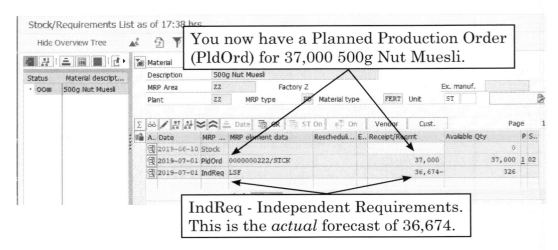

MRP looks at your forecast, looks at your ingredients list (or BOM), looks at the finished goods (including goods in-process or scheduled for production) and raw materials in stock, and then *plans* for which raw materials to order, how many of each raw material to order, and it creates a corresponding *planned* production order.

Quite Simply, MRP is Complicated

The above example simplifies MRP. Within the ERPsim Manufacturing Game, once you are several days or rounds into the simulation, it gets more complicated. Consider a more complicated ERPsim MRP run on Round 1, Day 20 with three products and an adjusted sales forecast of 100,000.

500g Nut Muesli	
Sales Forecast	100,000
Unsold Inventory	30,000
Scheduled Production	30,000
Raw Material Inventory	0

What is the quantity for the *planned production order*?

The forecast is for 100,000 finished 500g Nut Muesli. The current inventory is 30,000. There are 30,000 scheduled to be produced. MRP takes the forecast of 100,000, subtracts 30,000 of current inventory, and another 30,000 of in-process finished goods inventory.

The planned production order will be for 40,000 units of 500g Nut Muesli.

What is the quantity for each *purchase requisition*?

In order to produce 40,000 units of 500g Nut Muesli, with no raw material inventory, the raw material inventory for all 40,000 units must be purchased.

The five purchase requisitions for 40,000 500g Nut Muesli will show these quantities:

> 1 Small Box – 40,000 * 1 = 40,000
> 1 Small Bag – 40,000 * 1 = 40,000
> .175 kg Wheat – 40,000 * .175 = 7,000
> .175 kg Oats – 40,000 * .175 = 7,000
> .15 kg Nuts – 40,000 * .15 = 6,000

Wait, you said MRP is complicated...

Within ERPsim's master data, MRP calculates a minimum and maximim lot size for production runs. The minimum lot size is 16,000 units and the maximum is 48,000. This is where it gets complicated.

Go back to the example on the previous page. What if the unsold inventory level were 25,000 and the scheduled production were 25,000? The difference is 50,000. But with the lot size minimum and maximum, you'd end up with a production order of 48,000 and the remaining 2,000 would be rounded up to 16,000. You'd end up with a total order of 48,000 + 16,000 = 64,000!

Keeping up with the MRP calculations within the ERPsim Manufacturing Game can be a challenge. Remember those minimum and maximum lot sizes as you create your forecast and run MRP. With a minimum of 16,000, any production order under 16,000 will be rounded up to 16,000. If MRP calculates 48,001 products are required to meet the sales forecast, you'll end up with an order of 48,000 and an automatically adjusted production order of 16,000.

Spread this across twelve products and you may lose track of what's happening. If you go into the production process planning for and expecting this, it *shouldn't be* as complicated. This is also why it's good for all members of a team to completely understand the full production process. Don't leave understanding of production to one person. Everyone should understand the complexities of MRP!

In the "Real World" MRP is Very Complicated...

While the above example, and accompanying inset, is only slightly more complicated than the initial example, consider running MRP for a large company with 1,000s of products requiring 1,000s of raw materials per product.

It's in this situation that MRP within an ERP system shines, and increases efficiency. It's the simplicity of the manufacturing game which makes it easier to understand MRP, ERP systems, and how they are beneficial to a company's overall strategy.

Planning!

Remember, that MRP is nothing but *planning*. If all you do is run MRP, no raw materials will be ordered, and nothing will be produced. You just have a plan. Run it again, you have a new plan.

In order to manufacture something, you have to take the *plans* and convert those *plans* into actual orders.

Section 05 - Production

Manufacturing Finished Goods

After running MRP, you have a plan; nothing but a plan.

By running MRP, no raw materials will be ordered and nothing will be produced. Run MRP over and over, and all you have is a new set of plans.

But, when you're ready to execute the plan, how do you execute it?

Within SAP there are many ways to make this happen. This section will follow the process as it relates to the ERPsim Manufacturing Game. We'll use the ERPsim game as the example throughout this section, specifically referencing the Manufacturing Game's Job Aid and the actual transactions required to complete production within the simulation.

Converting Purchase Requisitions to Purchase Orders

While there are many ways to convert *Purchase Requisitions* to *Purchase Orders* within SAP, for the purposes of ERPsim's Manufacturing Game, one transaction will make this conversion: Create Purchase Orders, or, ME59N.

From the Job Aid:

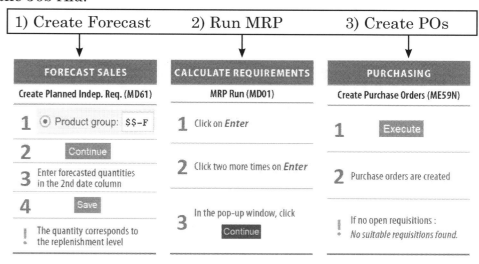

Creating a forecast was covered within the Sales Forecast section. Running MRP was covered within the MRP section. If you're not sure how we've reached this part of the process, re-read those two sections and then continue.

After the forecast has been entered, and after MRP has been executed, you have a list of *Purchase Requisitions*. By running the transaction ME59N, all of the open *Purchase Requisitions* are consolidated and converted into *Purchase*

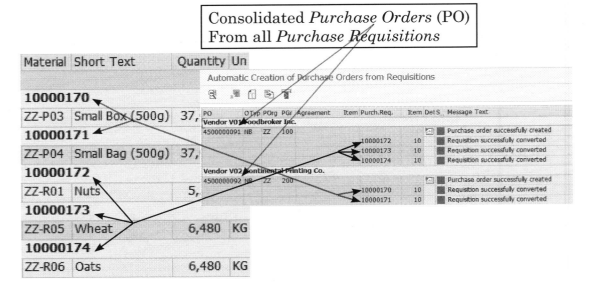

Orders.

Like running MRP, this is a simple transaction. And nothing really seems to happen. However, behind the scenes, open *Purchase Requisitions* have been converted into consolidated *Purchase Orders*.

The following is an abbreviated view of the consolidated PO for FoodBroker

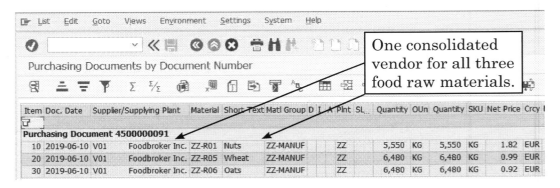

Inc.:

All of this happens automatically, and behind the scenes.

You Have Purchase Orders, Now What?

Within the "real world", these *Purchase Orders* would need to be officially placed as orders with the preferred vendor. This can take place electronically, by phone, by email, etc. The *Purchase Order* is simply a log of the original order, and the sales transaction. Many vendors expect a PO Number, the document number for this *Purchase Order,* within their internal *Sales Order.* Within the above example, the PO Number for Foodbroker Inc. is "4500000091". This number is typically referenced within all related communication between the vendor and organization placing the order.

However, while this is relevant and necessary within the "real world", it is not relevant within the ERPsim Manufacturing Game. Vendor management, submitting the order for raw materials, the receipt of those goods, and all related bookkeeping is automated.

Lead-time. Just Like the "Real World"

Few vendors provide goods instantly. Especially tangible goods like the raw materials within the ERPsim Manufacturing Game. Simulating the real world, POs have been placed with the vendor, and now you must wait for the vendor to ship and deliver those raw materials. This is referred to as vendor *Lead Time.*

Looking at the Manufacturing Game's Job Aid, we see that the lead time is

SUPPLIERS	
Lead time (days)	1-5
Payment time (days)	20

between 1 and 5 simulated days:
Note that this is the same lead-time you utilized within the Sales Forecast section to calculate your initial Sales Forecast.

Because you can't manufacture anything until the raw materials have been delivered, you need a report to tell you when they will be delivered, and a confirmation for the raw material delivery. ERPsim has created a customized SAP report which tracks *Purchase Orders.*

From the Job Aid:

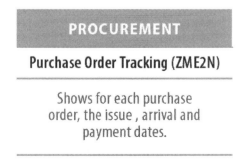

PROCUREMENT

Purchase Order Tracking (ZME2N)

Shows for each purchase order, the issue , arrival and payment dates.

Running transaction ZME2N brings up a customized report with your company's *Purchase Orders*.

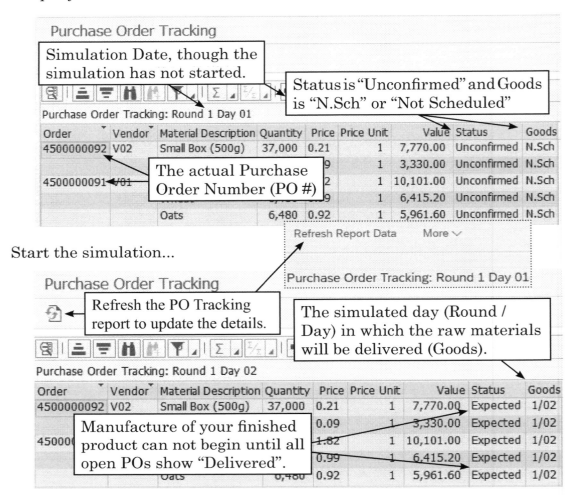

Start the simulation...

Note that "Goods", the raw materials, are due on Round 1, Day 2 (R1D2) of the simulation. Lead time is between 1 and 5 days. At this particular time, Foodbroker Inc. and Continental Printing will be delivering 1 day after the order was placed.

> Lead time within ERPsim's Manufacturing Game is randomly assigned from 1-5 days. However, within Round 1 during the first days of the simulation, lead time for both vendors is *always* set to 1 day. This allows all teams to receive their raw materials, start production, and start competing more quickly. About halfway through Round 1, lead time is randomly chosen from 1-5 days.

Because you cannot start manufacturing until all of the raw materials have been delivered, it's important to know exactly when they are available. While you could watch the inventory report, the Purchase Order Tracking Report will tell you exactly when those raw materials have been delivered.

Note the "Status" column within the report. With the above screen shot, the goods are listed as "Expected". Once the raw materials have been delivered, and are officially ready for production, the Status column will display "Delivered" clearly indicating delivery completion.

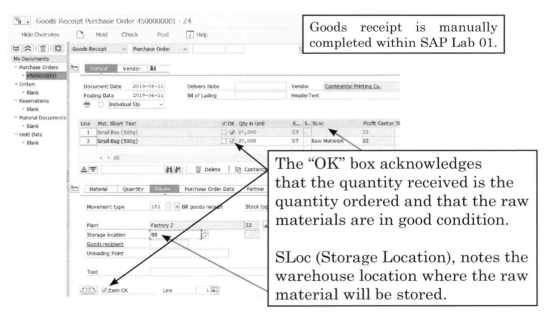

Purchase Order Tracking

Purchase Order Tracking: Round 1 Day 02

Order	Vendor	Material Description	Quantity	Price	Price Unit	Value	Status	Goods
4500000092	V02	Small Box (500g)	37,000	0.21	1	7,770.00	Delivered	1/02
		Small Bag (500g)	37,000	0.09	1	3,330.00	Delivered	1/02
4500000091	V01	Nuts	5,550	1.82	1	10,101.00	Delivered	1/02
		Wheat	6,480	0.99	1	6,415.20	Delivered	1/02
		Oats	6,480	0.92	1	5,961.60	Delivered	1/02

Receiving Raw Materials is Easy!

Again, ERPsim has simplified things. Within an actual company using SAP, someone would need to receive the raw materials, confirm their quantities and quality, and then compare the delivered materials and quantities to the original order.

Goods receipt is manually completed within SAP Lab 01.

The "OK" box acknowledges that the quantity received is the quantity ordered and that the raw materials are in good condition.

SLoc (Storage Location), notes the warehouse location where the raw material will be stored.

This *Goods Receipt* would directly reference the original *Purchase Order*.

Typically, one person would place the order while someone else would receive the order. This helps to cut down on internal fraud—one person orders, one person receives. Hopefully the two aren't in collusion.

Again, this is all automated while the simulation is running. When "Delivered" appears within the "Status" column of the Purchase Order Tracking Report, the raw materials are now in stock and available for production.

I Have My Raw Materials, Now What?

Remember that MRP plans for production. MRP looks at your sales forecast, then looks at your raw materials and in-process finished goods, and then creates a *plan* to produce enough products to meet your sales forecast.

This plan includes two different parts: *planned purchase orders* and *planned production orders*.

The planned purchase orders are the *Purchase Requisitions* that are converted into *Purchase Orders*. The planned production order is a *Planned Order* which can be converted into a *Production Order* once the raw materials are available.

Within SAP, there are many ways to convert *Planned Orders* into *Production Orders*. You can manually convert them, or you can automatically convert several orders at once. For speed and simplicity, the ERPsim Manufacturing Game prefers collective conversion of *Planned Orders*.

From the Job Aid:

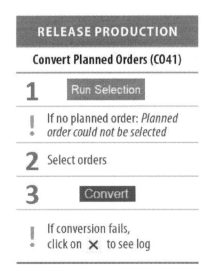

Following our example of 500g Nut Muesli:

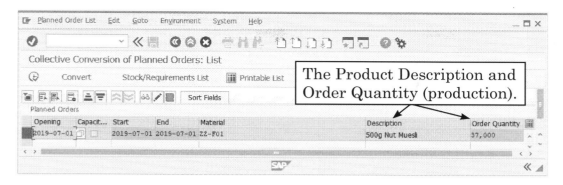

By clicking on the product's line and then clicking the "Convert" button, this *Planned Order* will be converted into a *Production Order*. If everything converts as expected (raw materials are in stock which match the quantity for the Planned Order), you'll receive a similar message to this:

> ✓ Planned order 222 was converted into production order 1000094

Going beyond our example, Transaction Code CO41 is designed to convert multiple *Planned Orders* at once. You can produce in a specific order by choosing and converting one product at a time.

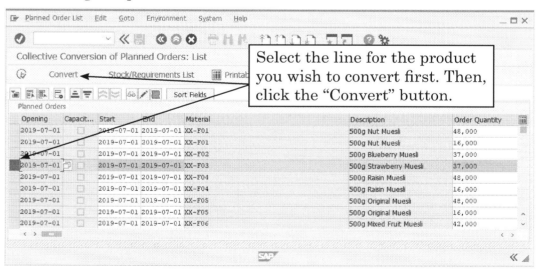

The Production Schedule will be updated based on the order in which you convert these *Planned Orders*. As part of a winning strategy within the ERPsim Manufacturing Game, it would be a good idea to confirm sales/marketing reports and current stock levels before converting. There's no point in rushing production of a product which is not selling and is currently in stock.

Once you convert the *Planned Orders*, they become *Production Orders*. Your

Production Schedule can be viewed using a customized report specifically used within the Manufacturing Game.

From the ERPsim Job Aid:

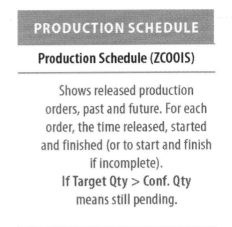

This transaction, ZCOOIS, brings up this custom report:

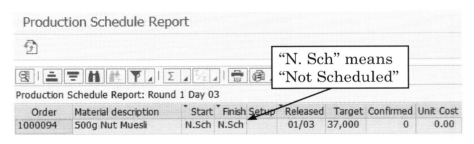

As simulated days progress, click the "refresh" button to follow production.

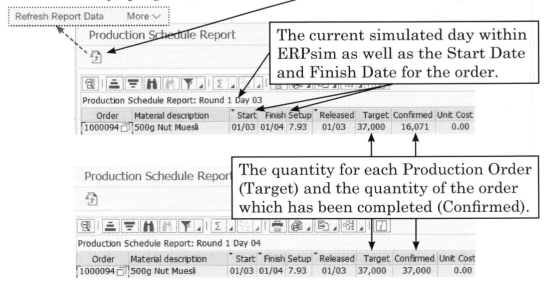

Of course, it's unlikely that you'd only be manufacturing one product with such a small forecast. ZCOOIS will, likely, be filled with multiple production orders:

Production Schedule Report

Production Order Numbers

Setup time between products

Production Schedule Report: Round 2 Day 01

Order	Material description	Start	Finish	Setup	Released	Target	Confirmed	Unit Cost
1000093	500g Mixed Fruit Muesli	N.Sch	N.Sch		02/01	32,000	0	0.00
1000092	500g Raisin Muesli	N.Sch	N.Sch			16,000	0	0.00
1000090	500g Blueberry Muesli	02/03	02/04	8.00	01/20	21		
1000091	500g Strawberry Muesli	02/02	02/03	8.00		37		
1000089	500g Nut Muesli	02/01	02/01	8.00		26,000	0	0.00
1000088	500g Blueberry Muesli	01/20	01/20	8.00	01/18	16,000	16,000	0.00
1000087	500g Nut Muesli	01/18	01/19	8.00		35,000	35,000	0.00
1000086	500g Original Muesli	01/16	01/17	8.00	01/07	37,000	37,000	0.00
1000084	500g Raisin Muesli	01/14	01/16	8.00		37,000	37,000	0.00
1000085	500g Mixed Fruit Muesli	01/12	01/14	8.00		37,000	37,000	0.00
1000083	500g Strawberry Muesli	01/10	01/12	8.00		37,000	37,000	0.00
1000082	500g Blueberry Muesli	01/08	01/10	8.00		37,000	37,000	0.00
1000081	500g Nut Muesli	01/07	01/08			37,000	37,000	0.00

Releasing Production – Strategically

Finished Goods become available for sale as each *Production Order* is confirmed. No sales take place without inventory in stock. There are no "backorders" within the ERPsim Manufacturing Game.

This is important to note as *Fixed Costs* (the daily expenses) continue even if you do not sell anything. A *Stock Out* of any product means that no sales of that product will take place until that product has been produced.

Reducing *Stock Outs* is part of a winning strategy within the ERPsim Manufacturing Game.

The order in which you convert each product is important; as is considering setup time between products. Does it make sense to release a production order for 16,000? With 8 hours of set-up time, your company will lose one third of a day's production just to manufacture 16,000 finished goods.

As you learn more about the production process, consider strategies which make for the most efficient production line as is possible.

You've Converted Production, When Do You Run MRP Again?

Remember that your Sales Forecast (from the Sales Forecast section) is based on what you plan to sell from MRP run to MRP run (MRP section). MRP calculates production orders based on the forecast and existing inventories. When do you run MRP again?

While various ERPsim Manufacturing Game strategies will lead to different MRP intervals, until you have a feel for your company's strategy, follow "Best Practices" for production:

> As soon as you finish converting all of your
> production orders, immediately run MRP.

Consistently ordering raw materials to be delivered just ahead of your scheduled production will lead to a more efficient production schedule, or higher productivity. This is important because if you wait until after the last scheduled production order, there will be no production during the vendor lead time, or 1-5 days. This concept becomes more important as we discuss productivity and your company valuation within a future section. For now, just know that after converting your *Planned Orders* (CO41), you should immediately run MRP (MD01) and convert your *Purchase Requisitions* (ME59N).

As an example, take a look at the following Purchase Order Tracking Report and the corresponding Production Schedule Report.

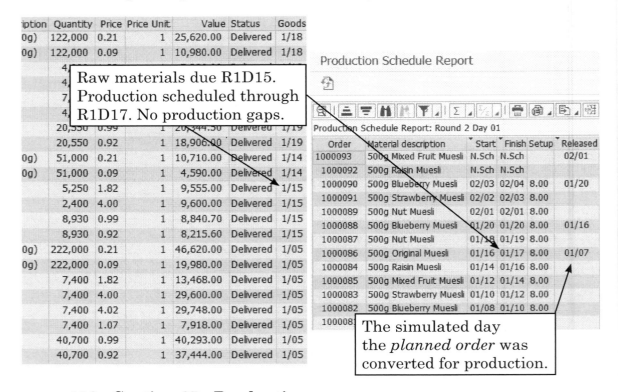

Note that the raw materials are due to be delivered *before* the production schedule ends. This should always be your goal.

No matter what's happening with sales, you'll always want your production running.

Watch for it – "No Suitable Purchase Requisitions Found"

In a previous example, we ordered enough raw materials to create 37,000 500g Nut Muesli. Once the raw materials were delivered, had we checked our inventory, we would have found that our raw material inventory was updated:

Inventory Report: Round 1 Day 08

SL	Material	Material description	Stock	Reserved	Unit
88	ZZ-P01	Large Box (1kg)	0	0	ST
	ZZ-P02	Large Bag (1kg)	0	0	ST
	ZZ-P03	Small Box (500g)	37,000	0	ST
	ZZ-P04	Small Bag (500g)	37,000	0	ST
	ZZ-R01	Nuts	5,550	0	KG
	ZZ-R02	Blueberries	0	0	KG
	ZZ-R03	Strawberries	0	0	KG
	ZZ-R04	Raisins	0	0	KG
	ZZ-R05	Wheat	6,475	0	KG
	ZZ-R06	Oats	6,475	0	KG

Within the ERPsim Manufacturing Game, "best practices" tell us that after converting our planned production orders to *Production Orders* (CO41), we should immediately repeat the production process.

Let's say that immediately after converting our orders (CO41), we run MRP (MD01), and then convert the purchase requisitions to purchase orders (ME59N).

Based on our sales forecast of 37,000, and raw material levels which EXACTLY match the raw material requirements for 37,000 500g Nut Muesli, and a Production Order for 37,000 500g Nut Muesli... what do you think will happen?

While MRP will run without an error, the next transaction (ME59N) will give you a message:

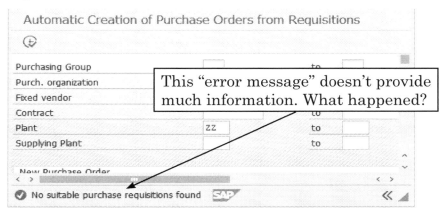

Automatic Creation of Purchase Orders from Requisitions

Purchasing Group
Purch. organization
Fixed vendor
Contract
Plant   ZZ
Supplying Plant
New Purchase Order

This "error message" doesn't provide much information. What happened?

No suitable purchase requisitions found

MRP takes everything into consideration—and only plans for what needs planning.

What happened? MRP did nothing. Nothing was planned. The sales forecast has been met—there is no need to order additional raw materials, there is no need to plan for any additional production for this finished product.

500g Nut Muesli	
Sales Forecast	37,000
Unsold Inventory	0
Scheduled Production	37,000
Raw Material Inventory*	37,000

With the forecast met, no purchase requisitions were created. When you tried to convert the purchase requisitions to purchase orders, there weren't any to convert. "No suitable purchase requisitions found".

*The raw material inventory is listed within inventory as "reserved". This means that one or more *planned orders* have been converted and the necessary raw materials have been allocated to the order(s). This raw material can not be used for the manufacture of any other product.

SL	Material	Material description	Stock	Reserved	Unit
88	ZZ-P01	Large Box (1kg)	0	0	ST
	ZZ-P02	Large Bag (1kg)	0	0	ST
	ZZ-P03	Small Box (500g)	37,000	37,000	ST
	ZZ-P04	Small Bag (500g)	37,000	37,000	ST
	ZZ-R01	Nuts	5,550	5,550	KG
	ZZ-R02	Blueberries	0	0	KG
	ZZ-R03	Strawberries	0	0	KG
	ZZ-R04	Raisins	0	0	KG
	ZZ-R05	Wheat	6,475	6,475	KG
	ZZ-R06	Oats	6,475	6,475	KG

MRP can be complicated.

Forecast to Production to Sales

The following details the process and the corresponding SAP transactions required to produce and sell a product.

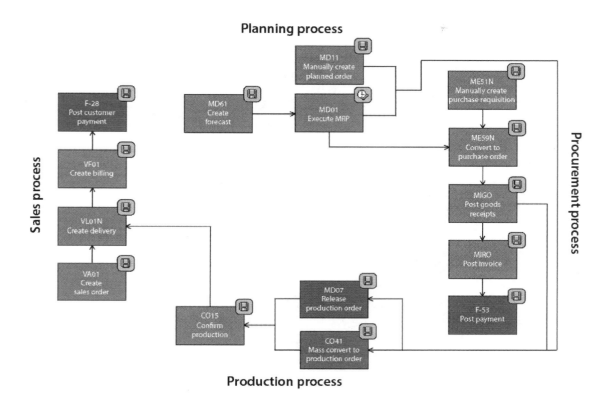

While the ERPsim Extended Manufacturing Game simulation is running, however, only four transactions are required:

1. MD61 – Create Forecast
2. MD01 – Execute MRP
3. ME59N – Convert to Purchase Order
4. CO41 – Mass Convert to Production Order

All other transactions, including sales, shipping, posting of payments, receipt of payments, and all other accounting transactions, are automatically completed by the simulation.

Is it Really This Easy?

The ERPsim Manufacturing Game has very simple processes in place. It is not that difficult to manufacture products, sell the products, and to make money.

Your company, Muesli AG, has numerous advantages over other "real world" manufacturers. For one, the company was built on top of SAP's processes and best practices. There was no need to map existing processes to SAP. Another advantage is that the company is extremely simple. A company with a handful of products is *highly unlikely* to use this version of SAP as their ERP system. This version of SAP is meant for organizations far more complicated than AG Muesli.

Is the ERPsim Manufacturing Game "Real World"?

Absolutely/Absolutely not! When you're running the simulation, you're interfacing with the actual out-of-the-box SAP that many of the world's largest organizations are using. Aside from some of the specific reports and programming required to simulate the passage of time, everything else is actual SAP transactions. These are the actual "real world" transactions and overall processes a large manufacturing company would be using.

But, as mentioned above, it's highly unlikely that a company with 12 products, one production line, and 3 distribution channels would use ERP software as complicated and as robust as this version of SAP.

ERPsim Provides a "Birds-Eye-View"

HEC Montréal has designed and programmed all of the ERPsim games to reduce the complexity of SAP. By making it easier and more simple to complete the various processes, it's easier to understand how ERP itself works across modules, and across functional areas within an organization. With simplicity, the processes themselves and how the data interacts becomes more clear.

When compared with many of the other options for learning ERP, and specifically SAP, ERPsim's games are the best for understanding the overall concepts, processes, and necessity of ERP—especially as it relates to the typical ERP end user.

With the simplicity of ERPsim, you can focus on strategy. How can your company be as profitable as possible while allocating your assets to show the best value to an outside investor?

Part III

Strategy!

Section 06 - Strategy?

Let's be realistic...

There are many options within the ERPsim Manufacturing Game. Some teams have different backgrounds from others and therefore think about strategy differently. There is no way that a section within a textbook could possibly explain "how to win".

But, what if it could? What if a header within this section were called "Here's the winning strategy!" Then what? Everyone uses the same strategy and... no one wins? No one learns?

So, let's be realistic. This section will discuss options. No one strategy will always win. No combination of strategies will always win. Every time you compete you'll want to try different strategies. Discuss with your team what worked, what didn't. Learn from game to game. Find your own strategy.

Your instructor can help you think through a strategy, but it is highly unlikely that he or she will *give you* the strategy. Winning the Manufacturing Game comes down to strategy. There's a reason why your instructor is using a strategic simulation within your course. If the positives and negatives of each strategy were given away, it would probably defeat the purpose of your learning experience.

Read, absorb, practice, ask questions. Find your team's winning strategy.

Company Valuation

Within the ERPsim Manufacturing Game, teams are ranked based on their company valuation. This valuation looks at your cumulative net income, your remaining liquid assets and your liabilities, and calculates the value of your company.

This is similar to how an investor may evaluate a company before investing. First, is the company profitable? Second, if the company were to shut down—how much "cash" does it have? Third, once all debts are paid, what's left?

In order to understand the ERPsim Manufacturing Game's company valuation, you need to have some basic understanding of accounting. Your Muesli Manufacturing Company runs accrual basis accounting—it does not run cash-basis accounting.

This is an important distinction when you consider net income, or your company's profitability.

$$\text{Revenue} - \text{Expenses} = \text{Net Income}$$

In accrual basis accounting, revenue is counted when the sale is made. Expenses are counted when the expense is made. Your net income is not related to when you receive payment from your customers, nor when you make payment to your vendors.

Net income is a measure of profitability within the organization. Cash is what your company uses to conduct business. Cash is also what an investor is interested in seeing. If your company goes out-of-business, how much cash do you have? How much cash are you expecting to receive (accounts receivable)? And, just as important, how much do you owe (loans, accounts payable)?

It doesn't matter how big your building is, how much inventory you are holding, how lean your manufacturing may be, nor the capacity of your production line. It's all about liquidity. If the company closes, how much cash will the investors get out of the company?

How do we Calculate Company Valuation?

Instead of jumping in here, let's start from the start: your company has to be profitable. Net income is the measure of your company's profitability. This factors directly into your company valuation. Before we talk about calculating the company valuation, let's work on making your company profitable.

Is Your Company Profitable?

Within ERPsim's Manufacturing Game, your company's profitability, or net income, is very important. It doesn't matter how much you've sold, your market share, nor your production capabilities; it's all about net income.

Without understanding your costs, it's unlikely that you'll be profitable.

How Do I Determine Costs in ERPsim's Manufacturing Game?

There's no easy way to do this. But there is a nice planning report which can help you get a good estimate. From there, it's up to you and your team to calculate more accurate per unit costs.

Transaction ZCK11, Product Cost Planning, updated througout the simulation:

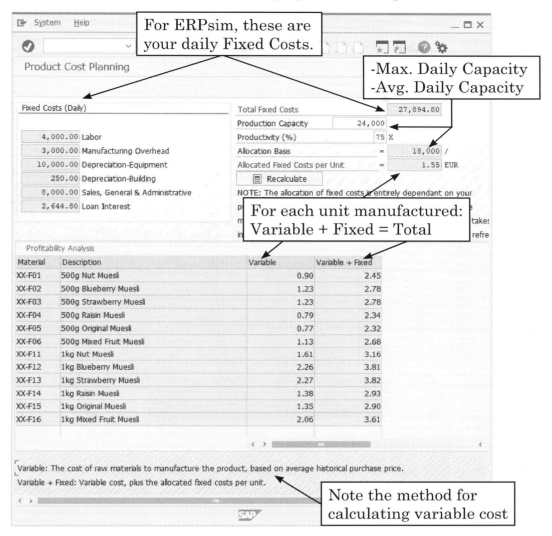

ZCK11 tracks your daily fixed costs and is updated if fixed costs change (investing in your capacity, changes to your loan's balance, etc.).

Your Company's Productivity and Profitability

Following the basic accounting premise that Revenue – Expenses = Profit (Net Income), to achieve positive net income your sales (revenue) must consistently exceed all costs (expenses). Increasing your profitability requires one of two things: increasing sales value (revenue) or reducing costs (expenses).

Increasing the value of your sales is easy—raise your price, but will it yield results? If you're the only company selling a certain product, raising your price may work. You may continue to sell your product at a more profitable rate. However, in a competitive market, if you try to raise your price you may need to invest in marketing—which also increases expenses. How much marketing will allow you to raise your price without reducing too much of your profits? All expenses must be closely monitored.

Reducing expenses can also increases your profitability.

Within the ERPsim Manufacturing Game, your variable costs include the costs of raw materials, marketing, warehousing capacity, and any other expenses you might incur through daily activites. Reduction of these expenses requires watching raw material prices, limiting warehouse capacity expenses, and making good business decisions throughout the game. Unfortunately, the cost of doing business often requires these variable costs—and there's not much you can do if your most profitable product includes a raw material which has increased in price throughout the simulation.

While there are ways to reduce your variable costs, which your company should explore, the most consistent way to reduce costs is to reduce your fixed costs.

Fixed costs within ERPsim include the following categories:

4,000.00	Labor
3,000.00	Manufacturing Overhead
10,000.00	Depreciation-Equipment
250.00	Depreciation-Building
8,000.00	Sales, General & Administrative
2,644.80	Loan Interest

With no changes to your loan amount or capacity, these fixed costs stay about the same throughout the simulation. While they are listed above as "daily", ERPsim automatically pays/expenses them every five days.

How do you Reduce a Fixed Cost?

While it's possible to pay down your loan (which reduces your loan interest expense), fixed costs are... fixed. No matter what you do, your fixed costs will stay about the same throughout the simulation.

There is, however, a way to *reduce* your per unit cost. It's quite simple to identify, but not so simple to execute: your fixed cost allocation basis. Increase your production / productivity and your per unit cost is reduced. The fixed costs are spread out across additional units, reducing fixed cost per unit.

Without investments, your production capacity starts at 24,000 units per day. This is reduced by mandatory setup time between products. Without investments, your starting setup time is 8 hours between products.

By default, the cost planning tool (ZCK11) starts at 75% productivity. This starting percentage presumes that your daily production will run 75% of the time, or 18 out-of-the 24 hours available each day for production. Your company's actual productivity will vary depending on your strategy. However, knowing your productivity percentage is crucial to determining the most profitable selling price for your products.

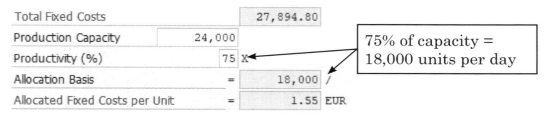

Total Fixed Costs		27,894.80
Production Capacity	24,000	
Productivity (%)	75 X	
Allocation Basis	=	18,000 /
Allocated Fixed Costs per Unit	=	1.55 EUR

75% of capacity = 18,000 units per day

Spreading the daily fixed costs across 75% of the starting capacity allocates fixed costs of 1.55€ per unit. The cost planning tool allows you to adjust this percentage to test various productivity scenarios. What happens if you produce at 50% of capacity?

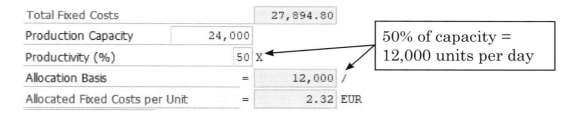

Total Fixed Costs		27,894.80
Production Capacity	24,000	
Productivity (%)	50 X	
Allocation Basis	=	12,000 /
Allocated Fixed Costs per Unit	=	2.32 EUR

50% of capacity = 12,000 units per day

Per unit costs increase from 1.55€ to 2.32€! It is unlikely that you'll be competitive with per unit allocated costs that are this high. But, what if you reach maximum productivity?

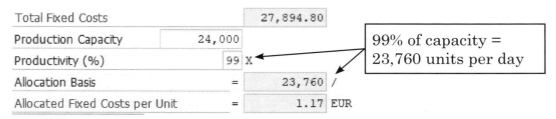

Total Fixed Costs		27,894.80
Production Capacity	24,000	
Productivity (%)	99 X	
Allocation Basis	=	23,760 /
Allocated Fixed Costs per Unit	=	1.17 EUR

99% of capacity = 23,760 units per day

While 100% is the maximum, ZCK11 only allows 2 digits—so we use 99%. But, what a difference this makes! Down from 1.55€ to 1.17€!

ZCK11 shows each of your twelve potential finished products, uses a historical average to calculate the variable cost (using the current BOM for each product), and then gives a unit Total Cost based on your Allocated Fixed Cost per Unit estimation.

		Allocated Fixed Costs per Unit	=	1.55
10,000.00	Depreciation-Equipment			
250.00	Depreciation-Building			
8,000.00	Sales, Gen...			
2,644.80	Loan Inte...			

Variable Cost + per Unit Allocated Fixed Costs
= estimated Total Unit Cost

into account a changed productivity assumption, and is n

Profitability Analysis

Material	Description	Variable	Variable + Fixed
XX-F01	500g Nut Muesli	0.90	2.45
XX-F02	500g Blueberry Muesli	1.23	2.78
XX-F03	500g Strawberry Muesli	1.23	2.78
XX-F04	500g Raisin Muesli	0.79	2.34
XX-F05	500g Original Muesli	0.77	2.32
XX-F06	500g Mixed Fruit Muesli	1.13	2.68
XX-F11	1kg Nut Muesli	1.61	3.16
XX-F12	1kg Blueberry Muesli	2.26	3.81
XX-F13	1kg Strawberry Muesli	2.27	3.82
XX-F14	1kg Raisin Muesli	1.38	2.93
XX-F15	1kg Original Muesli	1.35	2.90
XX-F16	1kg Mixed Fruit Muesli	2.06	3.61

Take the results from ZCK11 to create your pricing strategy. Remember, your revenues must exceed your expenses in order to be profitable. You must have your prices above cost!

Let's compare Team X above's costs to the 500g prices in VK32 for DC 12.

Current Prices					At 50% + Fixed	At 75% + Fixed	At 99% + Fixed
DCh1	Curr.	Materi...					
12	EUR	XX-F01...	2.35	EUR	3.22	2.45	2.07
12	EUR	XX-F02...	2.68	EUR	3.55	2.78	2.40
12	EUR	XX-F03...	2.57	EUR	3.55	2.78	2.40
12	EUR	XX-F04...	2.24	EUR	3.11	2.34	1.96
12	EUR	XX-F05...	3.06	EUR	3.09	2.32	1.94
12	EUR	XX-F06...	2.58	EUR	3.45	2.68	2.30

Is 50% productivity profitable (above cost) at the current prices? Only one of the products would sell above cost. And that's only profit of .03 per product sold. All other products, at 50% productivity, are being sold below cost. Even at 75% productivity these prices are questionable (below cost or tight margins).

At 99% productivity all six products are selling above cost, but, still at tight margins. Provided that production can keep up with sales at these prices, 99% productivity is certainly the most profitable of the above examples.

Indeed, as productivity increases, fixed costs are reduced. As fixed costs are reduced, and prices remain above cost, and those products can sell at that price, profitability can increase.

What's my Productivity?

Without using external Business Intelligence tools (such as Odata, discussed later!), you can only estimate your productivity during game play. You can estimate it by looking at your Production Schedule (ZCOOIS) and estimating the down-time you're experiencing on your production line. With 24 hours in a day, any days without productivity are 0/24 within your running productivity average. Switching between products also requires setup time, which means no productivity. This is listed as "Setup" within the Production Schedule Report:

Production Schedule Report

Production Schedule Report: Round 2 Day 01

Order	Material description	Start	Finish	Setup	Released	Target	Confirmed	Unit Cost
1000092	500g Raisin Muesli	N.Sch	N.Sch		02/01	16,000	0	0.00
1000093	500g Mixed Fruit Muesli	N.Sch	N.Sch			32,000	0	0.00
1000090	500g Blueberry Muesli	02/03	02/04	8.00	01/20	21,000	0	0.00
1000091	500g Strawberry Muesli	02/02	02/03	8.00		37,000	0	0.00
1000089		/01	02/01	8.00		16,000	0	0.00
1000088		/20	01/20	8.00	01/16	16,000	16,000	0.00
1000087	500g Nut Muesli	01/18	01/19	8.00		35,000	35,000	0.00
1000086	500g Original Muesli	01/16	01/17	8.00	01/07	37,000	37,000	0.00
1000084	500g Raisin Muesli	01/14	01/16	8.00		37,000	37,000	0.00
1000085	500g Mixed Fruit Muesli	01/12	01/14	8.00		37,000	37,000	0.00
1000		01/10	01/12	8.00		37,000	37,000	0.00
1000		01/08	01/10	8.00		37,000	37,000	0.00
1000081	500g Nut Muesli	01/07	01/08			37,000	37,000	0.00

Short production runs

Setup time between products

No production from R1D1-R1D6

Your exact productivity percentage can only be estimated here, but you can look through this production schedule and see some BIG productivity issues. The two biggest issues with this company's productivity include a few days with no production (R1D1 to R1D6) and the short production runs—with the full 8 hour setup time between product runs.

Consider an estimate of your daily productivity goal. Starting capacity is 24,000 per day, with 8 hours of setup time between products. To achieve a goal of 75% productivity, your production runs would need to be 18,000 per day. Looking at the above schedule, a production run of 16,000 with setup time of 8 hours immediately after will yield productivity less than 75%. How many production runs are less than 18,000, below 75%? Of the 13 listed production orders, 3 are less than 18,000. Only 9 of the production orders exceed the daily capacity of 24,000.

Without attempting to calculate the productivity % for this company, it is safe to say that it is below 75% productivity. It is unlikely that this company is achieving positive net income.

What is this company's actual productivity percentage? Between rounds, the ERPsim viewer provides calculated results (including productivity) for all participating teams. Ask your instructor for access to your simulation's viewer.

> The viewer only provides cumulative and per round information. Historical information is not kept in the viewer. Nor is this information available after the simulation has completed. If you are interested in this information, you'll want to copy and paste the information or take a screen shot and save it.

Looking at the end of round results for this particular team, which has been our example team throughout much of this text, it is not doing well:

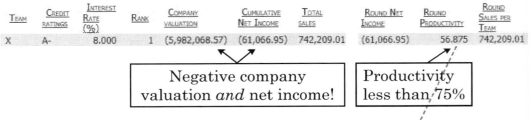

TEAM	CREDIT RATINGS	INTEREST RATE (%)	RANK	COMPANY VALUATION	CUMULATIVE NET INCOME	TOTAL SALES	ROUND NET INCOME	ROUND PRODUCTIVITY	ROUND SALES PER TEAM
X	A-	8.000	1	(5,982,068.57)	(61,066.95)	742,209.01	(61,066.95)	56.875	742,209.01

Negative company valuation *and* net income!

Productivity less than 75%

Let's plug this team's actual productivity into ZCK11 and see what happens:

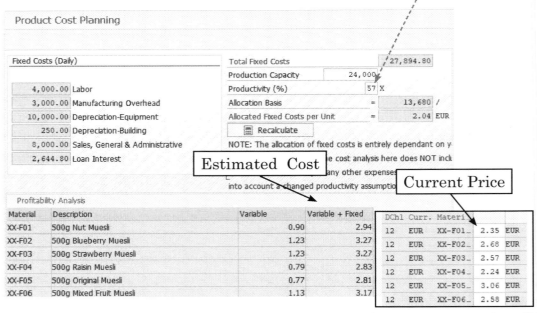

Product Cost Planning

Fixed Costs (Daily)

4,000.00	Labor
3,000.00	Manufacturing Overhead
10,000.00	Depreciation-Equipment
250.00	Depreciation-Building
8,000.00	Sales, General & Administrative
2,644.80	Loan Interest

Total Fixed Costs	27,894.80
Production Capacity	24,000
Productivity (%)	57 X
Allocation Basis =	13,680 /
Allocated Fixed Costs per Unit =	2.04 EUR

Recalculate

NOTE: The allocation of fixed costs is entirely dependant on y[...] e cost analysis here does NOT inc[...] any other expenses [...] into account a changed productivity assumptio[...]

Estimated Cost

Current Price

Profitability Analysis

Material	Description	Variable	Variable + Fixed
XX-F01	500g Nut Muesli	0.90	2.94
XX-F02	500g Blueberry Muesli	1.23	3.27
XX-F03	500g Strawberry Muesli	1.23	3.27
XX-F04	500g Raisin Muesli	0.79	2.83
XX-F05	500g Original Muesli	0.77	2.81
XX-F06	500g Mixed Fruit Muesli	1.13	3.17

DCh1	Curr.	Materi[...]		
12	EUR	XX-F01_	2.35	EUR
12	EUR	XX-F02_	2.68	EUR
12	EUR	XX-F03_	2.57	EUR
12	EUR	XX-F04_	2.24	EUR
12	EUR	XX-F05_	3.06	EUR
12	EUR	XX-F06_	2.58	EUR

Given their productivity within Round 1, only one of their products is selling above cost. All other products are selling ***below cost***. It is no surprise that this team has earned negative net income.

Productivity makes a huge difference to your company's bottom line. Always. Be. Producing.

Section 07 - Productivity

Sales and Productivity

Manufacturing of finished goods plays a substantial role in your company's profitability. No strategy will work without effective production. Why? Production is required for sales and sales are required for revenue. Expenses accumulate regardless of your sales (or lack there of). In order to keep revenue above expenses, you have to be producing. But, not just producing, you always need to be selling. Profitably.

Which leads to another item to note: While a company should Always. Be. Producing, they must also Always. Be. Selling.

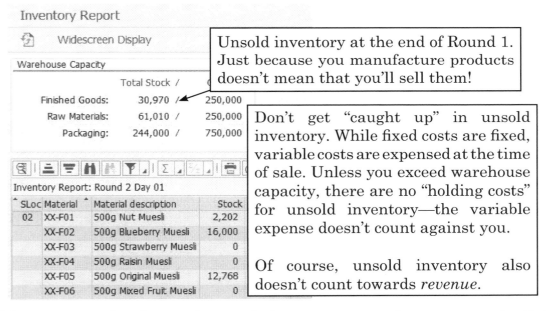

Unsold inventory at the end of Round 1. Just because you manufacture products doesn't mean that you'll sell them!

Don't get "caught up" in unsold inventory. While fixed costs are fixed, variable costs are expensed at the time of sale. Unless you exceed warehouse capacity, there are no "holding costs" for unsold inventory—the variable expense doesn't count against you.

Of course, unsold inventory also doesn't count towards *revenue*.

With company valuation as the metric for your company's success, productivity and sales aren't as easy as "revenue - expense = net income".

Before we look at ways to increase sales, let's continue discussing production.

Increasing Production / Productivity

There are a few ways to improve production / productivity within the ERPsim Manufacturing Game. One strategy is not any better than another. A combination of strategies may not be any better than no strategy. How you increase your production / productivity is up to you and your team. The best idea is to try them all during practices and find which ones work for you and your team. Just remember, each option has pros and cons, positives and negatives. You'll likely need to adjust some of your current processes to match the new strategy. And, remember, just because you can produce more doesn't mean that you can sell more. Producing more or otherwise increasing your productivity only makes sense if you can profitably sell the additional products.

> Don't be tempted to *stop* production because sales have stalled. Production should always be running. Sales just needs to figure out how to move more product. While they are figuring out what's happening, change your forecast as necessary and produce. Keep your productivity percentage as high as possible. Sales will catch up!

Investments in Capacity

Each company starts with 24,000 as their daily capacity. Each company can invest as much cash into capacity as they'd like. (If you run out of cash, your loan will increase.) That said, there are no guarantees that investing millions into capacity will turn into a winning company valuation. Each company should quantify their decision to upgrade their capacity—before they invest.

From the Job Aid:

INCREASE CAPACITY

G/L Account Posting (FB50)

1 Enter current date (F4) in *Document Date*

2	**1ˢᵗ Line**	**2ⁿᵈ Line**
Account	113300	11000
D/C	Credit	Debit
Amount	???	???

3 Click on *Enter*

4 Post

PRODUCTION CAPACITY	
Capacity (units/day)	24,000
Additional Capacity (€ per 1,000 units)	1 000 000**

**Investing in additional capacity will increase equipment depreciation costs

For every 1,000,000 euro you invest, you increase your capacity by 1,000.

> While this seems expensive, you're investing in a long-term asset. Long-term assets are depreciated over time, not immediately expensed. While you need to invest cash (short-term asset) into a long-term asset, the actual daily expense is a percentage of the actual investment.

Investments in Setup Time Reduction

Like capacity, each company begins with mandatory 8 hours of setup time between products. It does not matter what the two products are, there will be setup time between them. As an example, if you are manufacturing 1kg Nut Muesli and then choose to manufacture 500g Nut Muesli, there will be 8 hours of setup time between the two products.

The only way to avoid setup time is to constantly manufacture the same product.

If you choose to manufacture more than one product the entire game, you will have setup time between those products. Keep in mind that every hour that you aren't manufacturing is 1,000 products you could be manufacturing. Standard setup reduces total production by 8,000 units.

How do you reduce setup time? From the Job Aid:

SETUP TIME REDUCTION		
G/L Account Posting (FB50)		
1 Enter current date (F4) in *Document Date*		
2	1st Line	2nd Line
Account	113300	478000
D/C	Credit	Debit
Amount	???	???
3	Click on *Enter*	
4	Post	

SETUP TIME	
Setup time (hours)	**Investment** (€)
8	-
7	50 000
6	125 000
5	250 000
4	500 000
3	1 250 000

Setup time is calculated using a formula. This formula can be found within the Manufacturing Game Slides on the ERPsim Learning Portal (or from your instructor).

> Compared with investments in capacity, this does not seem very expensive. However, every euro you invest in setup time reduction is an *instant* expense, meaning, it comes right off of your net income. Invest 150,000 euro? Your net income drops 150,000 euro. Keep this in mind as you choose an investment strategy.

Both capacity and setup time investments should be quantified. You'll find that different strategies require different production improvements. Or, as you'll see next, no investment at all.

Don't Want to Invest in Production?

The only other way to increase productivity is to be more strategic with your production.

If you have too many days without production, you'll need to find a way to produce more often. This might be running the production process more often, or it may be adjusting your sales forecast.

If your issue is short production runs with long setup time between products, you have two options: skip converting small production runs, or adjust your forecast. Both options involve adjusting your sales forecast. Your goal should always be to sell what you're producing each day. Given your capacity and setup time limitations, you can't produce all twelve products each day, which means that you need to adjust your sales forecast based on which products are actually selling.

There are multiple ways to determine which products are selling and which are not. It is up to you and your team to analyze the many reports to decide this.

What About Sales?

Production and sales should be working together. You should sell about as much as you produce within one simulated day. You've now seen options for increasing productivity. But, what about sales?

The next section will discuss options for increasing sales.

Section 08 - Sales

Increasing Sales

As is true within this entire strategy discussion, there are no strategies which will always work. It all depends on the market, your company's strengths, and how you're investing your assets.

The following are options for increasing sales. Again, none are guaranteed.

Lower Your Price!

If your prices are above what the market is willing to pay, or above your competition, try lowering them. How much you lower your prices is up to your company's overall costs and strategies. However, the answer must be quantified. Calculate your cost before you adjust your price!

Increase Your Marketing!

Marketing is per product and regional—not by distribution channel. Keep in mind that "marketing" is all forms of advertisement: billboards, radio ads, TV ads, pop ups, keyword advertising, etc. If you're investing in marketing for multiple products within the same region, you're competing with yourself.

> Think about a soft drink company with multiple products. They may have a cola, a diet cola, and a white soda. All three products may be marketed within the same geographic area. One company, three ad compaigns. Large companies do this—but is it effective for you?

Quantify your marketing decisions. How much should you invest? How much investment impacts the market? Remember that this is a daily expense which comes right off of your net income. Quantify your decision.

Change Your Product!

This category has two options. The first is to stop producing whatever it is that isn't selling. This is fairly simple as there is no reason to sell all 12 products. In fact, by looking at both your sales reports and the market report, you should be able to tell which products are selling and selling profitably.

Comparing the sales reports, determine if you're selling profitably, or, if someone else has cornered the market for your product. If someone else is selling more profitably, stop selling that product. How? Reduce the sales forecast to "zero".

The other strategy is to literally change the product. Marketing isn't just promotion and price. It's also the product. Perhaps a new recipe is what you need to attract more sales?

From the Job Aid:

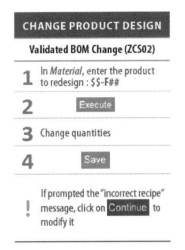

You can change the material quantities (BOM) for all 12 products. The changes must meet the minimum requirements for each product. From the Job Aid:

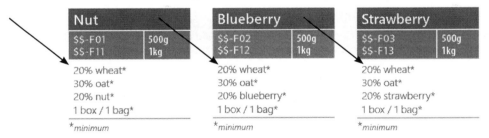

While you can't change the product itself (it must match the original label), you can adjust the quantities however you'd like. As an example, change 500g Strawberry so that it has 60% strawberry, 20% wheat, and 20% oat.

Remember that the product itself is marketing. Within the above example, perhaps having more strawberry than your competitors is enough to sell more product? There's only one way to find out: produce it and see what happens. If you sell more, it worked!

Quantify Your Decisions!

Most important in increasing sales is quantifying your decisions. Don't just change prices or increase marketing without a plan. Calculate and quantify!

Section 09 - Your Valuation

Company Valuation

Your production is optimized, sales are steady, how do you win?

Rankings within the ERPsim Manufacturing Game are based on your company's valuation. As mentioned earlier, this valuation is similar to how an investor may evaluate a company before investing. First, is the company profitable? Second, if the company were to shut down—how much "cash" does it have? Third, once all debts are paid, what's left?

The calculation itself is fairly straight-forward, but winning is not quite as straight-forward. The following will give an overview of the ERPsim Manufacturing Game's company valuation calculation.

> This text gives an overview of the calculation. The ERPsim Manufacturing Game's Participant's Guide (available on the ERPsim Lab's website) gives greater detail, depth, and explanation of the valuation. Read through the Participant's Guide for more information.

In order to explain the company valuation, we'll deconstruct Company X's one round performance. First, let's look at the calculated valuation from the end of round results:

FINANCIAL STATEMENTS - R1

Team	Credit Ratings	Interest Rate (%)	Rank	Company Valuation	Cumulative Net Income
X	A-	8.000	1	(5,982,068.57)	(61,066.95)

Open the combined balance sheet and income statement using transaction F.01. Open the folders for "Current assets" and "Current liabilities".

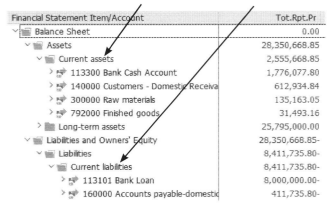

Financial Statement Item/Account	Tot.Rpt.Pr
Balance Sheet	0.00
Assets	28,350,668.85
Current assets	2,555,668.85
113300 Bank Cash Account	1,776,077.80
140000 Customers - Domestic Receiva	612,934.84
300000 Raw materials	135,163.05
792000 Finished goods	31,493.16
Long-term assets	25,795,000.00
Liabilities and Owners' Equity	28,350,668.85-
Liabilities	8,411,735.80-
Current liabilities	8,411,735.80-
113101 Bank Loan	8,000,000.00-
160000 Accounts payable-domestic	411,735.80-

Remember what an investor wants to see: liquidity (cash and accounts receivables) and liabilities (loan, accounts payable). None of a company's other assets (current or long-term) are considered within this calculation.

The first part of the valuation is to calculate the company's debt load. This, simply, calculates how much debt a company has on its books. Add the current liabilities together, and subtract the liquid current assets.

(Bank Loan + Accounts Payable) - Cash - Accounts Receivables

This result is the company's debt load.

Bank Loan	€ 8,000,000.00
Accounts Payable	€ 411,735.80
Cash	€ (1,776,077.80)
Accounts Receivables	€ (612,934.84)
Debt Load	€ 6,022,723.16

The company's debt load is used to find the company's risk rate. (For more information about this, look online or read the Manufacturing Game's Participant's Guide.)

The debt load is looked up within a table to determine the company's risk differential.

Debt Loading		Rating	Risk Differential
€	-	AAA+	3.00%
€	1,000,000	AA+	3.75%
€	2,000,000	AA	4.00%
€	3,000,000	AA-	4.25%
€	4,000,000	A+	4.75%
€	5,000,000	A	5.00%
€	6,000,000	A-	5.25%
€	7,000,000	BBB+	5.75%
€	8,000,000	BBB	6.00%
€	9,000,000	BBB-	6.25%
€	10,000,000	BB+	6.75%

Company X, with a calculated debt load of €6,022,723, returns with an A- rating, and a 5.25% risk differential. Add that differential to the game's standard market risk rate of 7%.

Risk Rating	A-
Risk Rate	12.25%

Next, check the ending net income.

Net Income (Loss)	61,066.95-
Calculated Result	61,066.95-

Negative net income! This value is used to calculate this company's annual net income. ERPsim calculates this by determining how many rounds have been completed, which it considers one month. For company X we've completed one round, or one month.

The calculation is: net income * (12 / # of rounds completed)

Cumulative Net Income	€	(61,066.95)
Annual Net Income	€	(732,803.40)

Using the risk rate, we calculate the company valuation.

Annual Net Income / Risk Rate = Company Valuation

-732,803.40 / 12.250% = -5,982,068.57

FINANCIAL STATEMENTS – R1

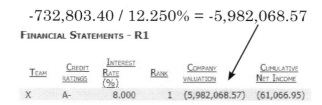

TEAM	CREDIT RATINGS	INTEREST RATE (%)	RANK	COMPANY VALUATION	CUMULATIVE NET INCOME
X	A-	8.000	1	(5,982,068.57)	(61,066.95)

Again, this is a quick overview of the company valuation calculation. If you are interested in a more detailed explanation, read through the ERPsim Manufacturing Game Participant's Guide.

In addition, you will find videos discussing company valuation and quantifying strategies on this textbook's website: www.TheCourseWebsite.com

Additional Company Valuation Calculation

It will be within your best interest to understand how company valuation is calculated. Understanding the calculation will help guide your strategy throughout gameplay. Let's walk through the calculation using F.01's report:

∨ 📊 Balance Sheet	0.00
∨ 📊 Assets	29,464,368.43
∨ 📊 Current assets	4,663,118.44
> 📑 113300 Bank Cash Account	3,051,834.13
> 📑 140000 Customers - Domestic Receiva	1,263,527.52
> 📑 300000 Raw materials	295,546.79
> 📑 792000 Finished goods	52,210.00
> 📊 Long-term assets	24,801,249.99
∨ 📊 Liabilities and Owners' Equity	29,464,368.43-
∨ 📊 Liabilities	8,778,850.00-
∨ 📊 Current liabilities	8,778,850.00-
> 📑 113101 Bank Loan	8,000,000.00-
> 📑 160000 Accounts payable-domestic	778,850.00-
> 📊 Equity	20,685,518.43-
> 📊 Income Statement	685,518.43-
∨ 📊 Net Income (Loss)	685,518.43
• Calculated Result	685,518.43

First, calculate the team's debt load. This is the formula:

$$(\text{Bank Loan} + \text{Accounts Payable}) - \text{Cash} - \text{Accounts Receivables}$$

The calculated debt load:

Bank Loan	€ 8,000,000.00
Accounts Payable	€ 778,850.00
Cash	€ (3,051,834.13)
Accounts Receivables	€ (1,263,527.52)
Debt Load	€ 4,463,488.35

The debt load is looked up within a table to determine the company's risk differential.

Net Debt		Rating	Risk Differential
€	-	AAA+	3.00%
€	1,000,000	AA+	3.75%
€	2,000,000	AA	4.00%
€	3,000,000	AA-	4.25%
€	4,000,000	A+	4.75%
€	5,000,000	A	5.00%
€	6,000,000	A-	5.25%
€	7,000,000	BBB+	5.75%

A calculated debt load of €4,463.488.35 returns with an A+ rating, and a 4.75% risk differential. Add that differential to the game's standard market risk rate of 7% for an 11.75% risk rate.

Risk Rating	A+
Risk Rate	11.75%

Next, determine the number of rounds completed:

Inventory Report: Round 2 Day 01 ← From any ERPsim Report

R2D1 means one round (R1D1 through R1D20) has been completed.

Determine cumulative net income from F.01:

∨ 📦 Net Income (Loss)	685,518.43
• Calculated Result	685,518.43

Calculate annual net income.

The calculation is: net income * (12 / # of rounds completed)

Cumulative Net Income	€ 685,518.43
Annual Net Income	€ 8,226,221.16

Using the risk rate, calculate this company's valuation.

$$\text{Annual Net Income} / \text{Risk Rate} = \text{Company Valuation}$$

$$685{,}518.43 / 11.75\% = 70{,}010{,}392.85$$

> Setup time reduction requires a slightly adjusted company valuation formula. The following pages include a discussion on how setup time reduction adjusts the company valuation calculation.

How Do I Increase My Company's Valuation?

Increase your net income and/or decrease your debt load. There are only five numbers from your company's financial statements which factor into the calculation. Three should be increased, and two should be decreased.

Decrease These	Increase These
• Accounts Payable • Bank Loan	• Accounts Receivable • Net Income • Cash

All strategies should be quantified or otherwise qualified so that they, in one way or another, increase your company valuation.

> This textbook includes instructions for completing a "real-time" company valuation calculator. It is in your best interest to explore this section, and Odata connectivity, to quantify / qualify your strategies.

"Hidden" Expenses Impact Net Income!

The ERPsim Manufacturing Game uses SAP, its standard processes, and standard transactions. The only non-standard transactions are either for customized reports or for "spoofing" the system to show the passage of simulated time. SAP does not provide updates nor notifications when something changes.

Given all of this, there is no fanfare, nor warning message, nor any other notification when your company has various expenses. The "daily costs" from ZCK11 are expensed and paid every 5 days. There is no notification for this—it's all automated and behind-the-scenes. And every expense impacts net income.

Are the expenses actually hidden? Not really. They can all be found within your combined financial statements in transaction F.01. But, if you don't look for them, or don't account for them, you don't know that they are there.

The following pages note some "hidden" expenses to watch.

Marketing Expenses

While marketing is a strategic choice, how much it's costing your company is not always transparent. Confirm your marketing expenses within F.01:

Remember, marketing is an expense which comes right off of your net income. Your team should always quantify your marketing decisions, and, your team should determine your marketing's effectiveness and ROI.

Warehouse Expenses

When you exceed your warehouse capacity, you are automatically billed for additional warehouse space. There are no error messages, no fanfare, nothing.

From the job aid:

STORAGE CAPACITY AND COSTS		
Product type	Current space	Cost per additional 50,000 units*
Finished product	250,000 boxes	€500/day
Raw materials	250,000 kg	€1 000/day
Packaging (bags and boxes)	750,000 units	€100/day

*Billed automatically

It's up to you and your group to monitor your warehouse capacity expenses. Your current warehouse stock and capacity are within the inventory report, ZMB52.

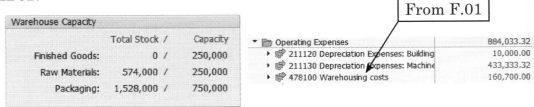

> Warehouse storage capacity and production capacity are two different things. An investment in production capacity will increase how many units you can manufacture within a day. It does not change your warehouse storage capacity. Instead, as necessary, the simulation automatically "rents" additional storage space to meet your warehouse needs. These are the daily costs listed on the job aid (above).

Setup Time Reduction

Setup time reduction is an expense. You're, essentially, paying a consultant to help you with lean manufacturing techniques. Payments to consultants are expensed at the time the services are rendered. Within ERPsim, this expense takes place as soon as you save the FB50 transaction, and is reflected within your company's cumulative net income.

Setup Time Reduction — And Company Valuation

Consider the company valuation calculation. It extrapolates your cumulative net income to calculate your annual net income. If you've invested in setup time reduction... your cumulative net income has been reduced by this expense. This is typically a one-time expense which should not count against your calculated annual net income. If you use the previous Company Valuation formula *and* you've invested in setup time reduction, your annual net income is lower than it should be.

ERPsim makes a special Company Valuation calculation for those companies that have chosen to invest in Setup Time Reduction.

What's the difference? Instead of using the calculated net income from F.01, first it adds the total setup time investment back into your net income, calculates your annual net income, and then subtracts the total setup time investment from your annual net income.

As an example, we'll revist the previous "additional company valuation calculation" presuming that this company made a 100,000 euro investment in setup time reduction. Within the example, 1 round has been completed.

The debt load calculation and risk rate is exactly the same:

Bank Loan	€ 8,000,000.00
Accounts Payable	€ 778,850.00
Cash	€ (3,051,834.13)
Accounts Receivables	€ (1,263,527.52)
Debt Load	€ 4,463,488.35

Risk Rating	A+
Risk Rate	11.75%

From here, the "Annual Net Income" calculation is different:

∨ Net Income (Loss)	685,518.43
* Calculated Result	685,518.43

((net income + setup investment) * (12 / # of rounds)) - setup investment

Cumulative Net Income	€ 685,518.43
Setup Time Investment	€ 100,000.00
Revised Net Income	€ 785,518.43
Annual Net Income	€ 9,326,221.16

From there, using the risk rate, calculate the valuation:

Annual Net Income / Risk Differential = Company Valuation

785,518.43 / 11.75% = 79,372,094.98

By treating setup time reduction as a special expense, the company valuation is more fairly calculated for teams that have investment in setup time reduction.

It is, however, still an expense. And without checking F.01, you may not realize that it is taking away from your net income.

Check F.01 Often!

Your team should make a habit of checking F.01 for your current account balances. Sometimes a simple mistake can create major problems. As an example, what if you accidentally add a "zero" to the end of your marketing investment? Suddenly your 100 euro marketing is 1,000 euros, per day. A check of F.01 will help catch these errors before they cost you too much net income.

Quantifying Strategies

All ERPsim strategies can and should be quantified. At the very least, calculate a return on investment for any additional expenses you may incur.

As an example, perhaps warehouse expenses can be justified? Maybe holding on to extra inventory (raw or finished goods) can make your company more profitable? You'll need to quantify this.

What about marketing expenses? How much is too much? You'll need to quantify this.

No matter what, a statement within your group like, "I think we should lower the price." is not a quantified statement. How much should you lower your price? Why? Calculate your strategy, see what happens, and compare the actual results with your calculations.

All strategic decisions within ERPsim should be quantified.

> While there are numerous ways to acquire data from ERPsim to quantify (or qualify) your strategies, this textbook includes multiple sections on using OData to provide real-time analytics of your ERPsim data. Check the table of contents for this section.
>
> All ERPsim clients and servers are OData compatible!

Part IV

OData
for
Strategy

Section 10 - OData

What is OData?

OData (Open Data Protocol) allows easy and universal access to data. Many data-oriented software packages (such as Microsoft Excel and Tableau) include OData as one of their standard data acquisition protocols.

The technical background required to understand how and why OData works with S/4 HANA is outside the scope of this textbook. For our purposes, realize that it's the protocol which allows us "real-time" access to ERPsim data.

For more information about OData, please visit its website: odata.org

OData and ERPsim

Throughout this textbook, a common message has been noted: ERPsim strategies should be quantified or otherwise qualified. While there are numerous ways to do this, for real-time analytics, OData is the best option.

Some examples of fairly straight-forward prescriptive and descriptive analytics which can be helpful within the ERPsim Manufacturing Game are included within this textbook.

These step-by-step guides are not meant to be exhaustive. Instead, they are examples to help you start your journey into quantified / qualified ERPsim strategies.

Connecting to ERPsim's OData

While connecting to ERPsim's OData isn't all that difficult, there are multiple steps to be completed before you can even analyze the data. If you are unfamiliar with data acquisition techniques and processes, this may be more challenging.

The good news is that once you get some practice connecting, it becomes much easier. In other words, don't quit from frustration after trying to set up your connection. It requires multiple steps, and, it gets easier with practice!

> While this textbook will walk you through acquiring ERPsim data using OData, it is impossible to predict where you may have trouble.
>
> If you are stuck, contact your instructor.

Before you Begin!

Before you start, make sure that you have the following information:

- Your ERPsim Server, Client, UserID and password
- At least 1 round of ERPsim data within the above server / client
- The OData specific username and password for the above server
    - This is NOT your ERPsim user ID ($1, $2, etc.)
- The URL for the OData Application URI Builder

Unless you are using SAP Fiori as your ERPsim interface, the above logon information and links will be provided to you by your instructor. Without SAP Fiori, there is no other way to acquire the above information.

OData Connection Information Within SAP Fiori

If you are using SAP Fiori and have completed at least one round of the ERPsim Manufacturing Game, you can easily find your OData connection information.

From the SAP Fiori ERPsim Dashboard's Home screen:

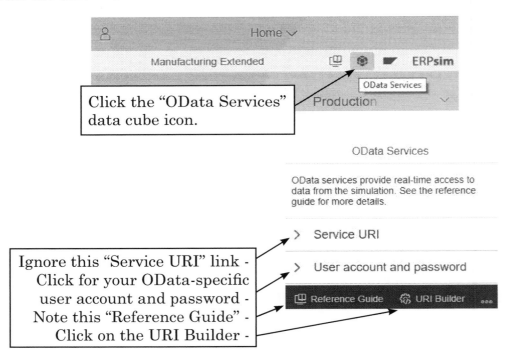

The OData URI Builder

The purpose of this URI Builder is to provide your analytics software with either a direct or indirect link to your ERPsim data view. Some software, such as Microsoft Excel will allow you to choose between various data views. Other software, such as Tableau, requires a link to a specific data view. The URI Builder will help you create the correct URI for your needs.

When you visit the OData URI Builder it will immediately prompt you for a Username and Password. This is NOT your ERPsim user ID and password!

Be sure to use the OData-specific username and password provided to you by your instructor, or, from within SAP Fiori.

The Username and Password is OData-specific!

Once you have logged on, you will be taken to the ERPsim OData Services URI Builder. This URI Builder will create the URI that you will use to connect your ERPsim data to your analytics software (MS Excel, Tableau, etc.)

What you do from here will entirely depend on what you plan to do next with OData. You can't break anything so don't hesitate to try things.

What can you do with ERPsim OData?

If it's data within the ERP system (your ERPsim data), you can analyze it. The options are endless. If you'd like to see the most up-to-date instructions and data view guides, you'll want to take a look at the ERPsim OData "Reference Guide". While this textbook is current as of its publication data, the ERPsim "Reference Guide" is always being updated.

For up-to-date information about ERPsim and OData, visit the ERPsim Learning Portal. Within your browser, visit: erpsim.hec.ca

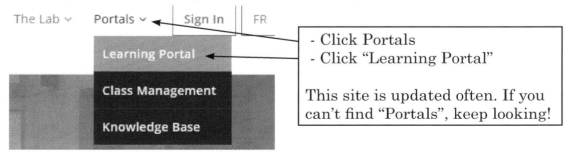

- Click Portals
- Click "Learning Portal"

This site is updated often. If you can't find "Portals", keep looking!

You'll be prompted to "Log in". This is the username and password you set up when you paid for ERPsim. This is NOT your ERPsim user ID and password.

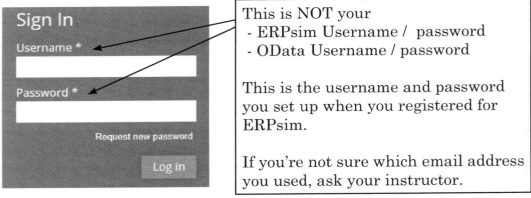

This is NOT your
- ERPsim Username / password
- OData Username / password

This is the username and password you set up when you registered for ERPsim.

If you're not sure which email address you used, ask your instructor.

If you are not automatically taken to the "Learning Portal", click on the "Learning Portal" link under "Portals".

While this site is often updated, the OData connectivity information *should* be listed under Content -> Books and Guides

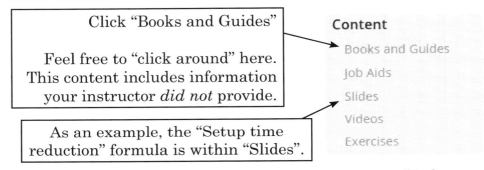

Click "Books and Guides"

Feel free to "click around" here. This content includes information your instructor *did not* provide.

As an example, the "Setup time reduction" formula is within "Slides".

While it may change heading names (improvise!), click on "Reference Guide: ERPsim for SAP HANA".

This Reference Guide is constantly updated with new instructions, data views, data view explanations, and, instructions for new analytics tools.

YOU WILL NEED TO IMPROVISE

There are numerous versions and configurations of operating systems (Windows, Mac, Linux, etc.) and analytics software (MS Excel, Tableau, SAP Lumira, etc.). It is improbable that screen shots within these OData instructions will exactly match your version and configuration.

If you are stuck, contact your instructor (or Google it!).

Unlike this textbook, this ERPsim Portal is always the most up-to-date resource for everything ERPsim. Not sure what to do with your data? What it means? How to access it within another software package?

Always start within the Learning Portal. It's always up-to-date!

Connecting Analytics Software to ERPsim OData

Want to create some sort of predictive, prescriptive or descriptive analytics tool? The following are the general instructions for making the OData connection to ERPsim within MS Excel and Tableau. If you are using different software, you will need to improvise from these instructions. Google it! Ask your instructor!

Do keep in mind that "real time" analytics require an active simulation. Your connection will need to be set up every time you start a new simulation with a new client and / or company code.

Creating an OData Connection with MS Excel

At this point, you should have reached the "URI Builder" site provided to you by either your instructor or within SAP Fiori. If you have not accessed that site, go back to the start of these instructions, log on, and come back to these instructions.

You should also have an idea of which data view you plan to analyze. If you will be following the instructions from this textbook, this data view will be provided for you. Otherwise, you may explore the data views, or, look through the ERPsim Reference Guide for an explanation of the various data views.

Because this is MS Excel, the basic ERPsim data view from the URI Builder will work for us.

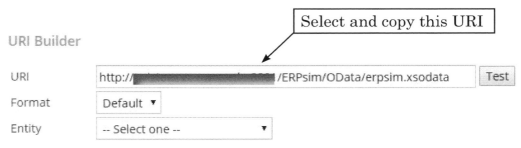

From within a blank MS Excel workbook, create a new data connection.

> There are numerous versions and configurations of MS Excel, so you may need to improvise. Look online, click "Help", etc. The following screenshots are from Excel Office 365 Version 1808 running on the 64 bit version of Windows 10 Pro, Build 1803.
>
> If you are stuck, contact your instructor (or Google it!).

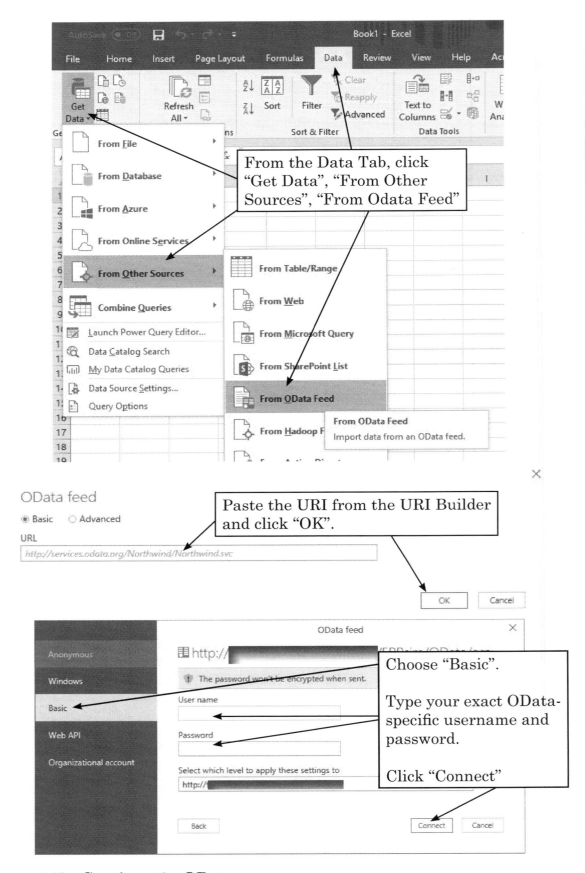

From the Data Tab, click "Get Data", "From Other Sources", "From Odata Feed"

From OData Feed
Import data from an OData feed.

OData feed

⦿ Basic   ◯ Advanced

URL

http://services.odata.org/Northwind/Northwind.svc

Paste the URI from the URI Builder and click "OK".

OK   Cancel

OData feed

http://   /FRPsize/OData/...

⚠ The password won't be encrypted when sent.

User name

Password

Select which level to apply these settings to

http://

Back   Connect   Cancel

Choose "Basic".

Type your exact OData-specific username and password.

Click "Connect"

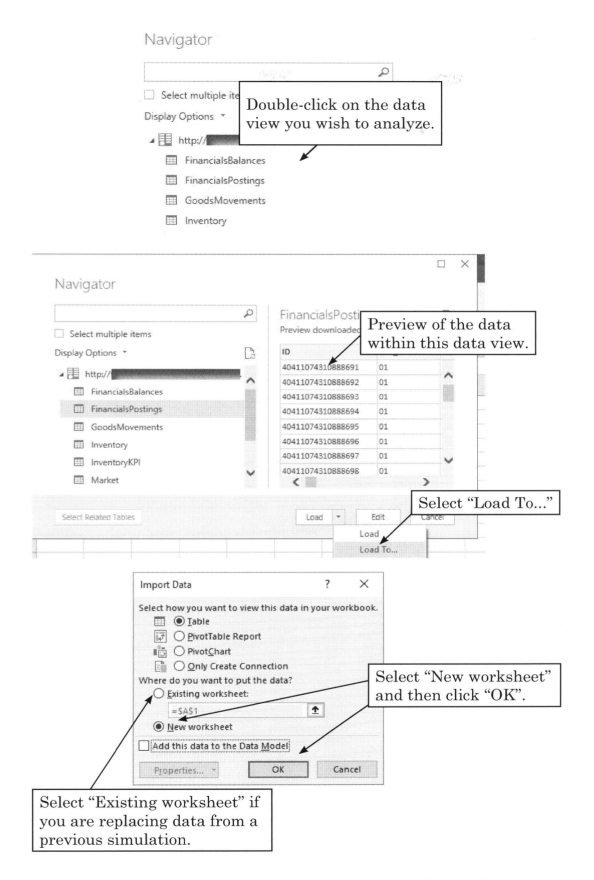

Navigator

Double-click on the data view you wish to analyze.

Select multiple ite

Display Options ▾

▲ ⊞ http://

⊞ FinancialsBalances

⊞ FinancialsPostings

⊞ GoodsMovements

⊞ Inventory

Navigator

Select multiple items

Display Options ▾

▲ ⊞ http://

⊞ FinancialsBalances

⊞ FinancialsPostings

⊞ GoodsMovements

⊞ Inventory

⊞ InventoryKPI

⊞ Market

FinancialsPosti

Preview downloaded

Preview of the data within this data view.

ID	
40411074310888691	01
40411074310888692	01
40411074310888693	01
40411074310888694	01
40411074310888695	01
40411074310888696	01
40411074310888697	01
40411074310888698	01

Select "Load To..."

Select Related Tables   Load ▾   Edit   Cancel

Load

Load To...

Import Data   ?   ✕

Select how you want to view this data in your workbook.

⊞ ● Table

◯ PivotTable Report

◯ PivotChart

◯ Only Create Connection

Where do you want to put the data?

◯ Existing worksheet:

=A1   ⬆

● New worksheet

☐ Add this data to the Data Model

Properties... ▾   OK   Cancel

Select "New worksheet" and then click "OK".

Select "Existing worksheet" if you are replacing data from a previous simulation.

Creating an OData Connection with MS Excel   149

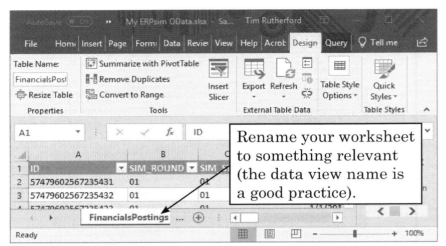

No clue what to do in MS Excel?

The textbook will walk you through some fairly easy MS Excel ERPsim spreadsheet data models using OData. Unfortunately, teaching the basics of MS Excel spreadsheet data models is outside the scope of this textbook.

The instructions presume general understanding of prescriptive and descriptive analytics. If you have software questions, look online or ask your instructor. There are many other resources available for learning this software!

Creating an OData Connection with Tableau

At this point, you should have reached the "URI Builder" site provided to you by either your instructor or within SAP Fiori. If you have not accessed that site, go back to the start of these instructions, log on, and come back to these instructions.

You will also need to know which data view you plan to analyze. If you will be following the instructions from this textbook, this data view will be provided for you. Otherwise, you may explore the data views, or, look through the ERPsim Reference Guide for an explanation of the various data views.

Because this is Tableau, you will need to use the URI Builder to create a link to an exact data view.

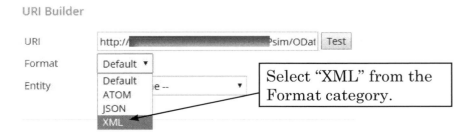

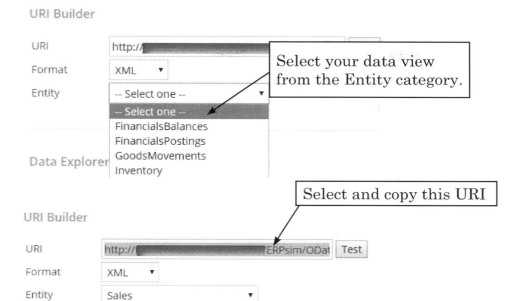

Select your data view from the Entity category.

Select and copy this URI

There are numerous versions and configurations of Tableau, so you may need to improvise. Look online, click "Help", etc. The following screenshots are from Tableau Desktop Professional Edition, 2019.1.3 64 bit running on the 64 bit version of Windows 10 Pro, Build 1803.

If you are stuck, contact your instructor (or Google it!).

Open a new Tableau Worksheet.

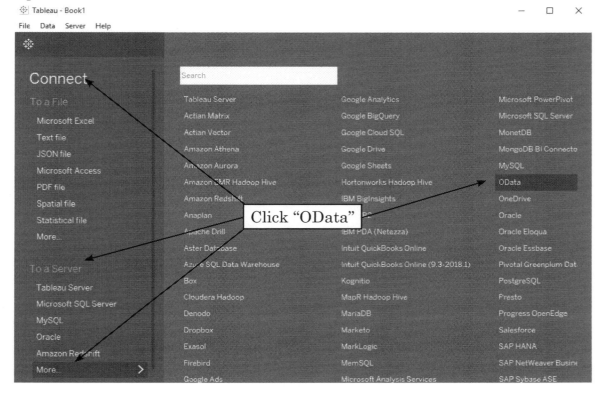

Click "OData"

OData

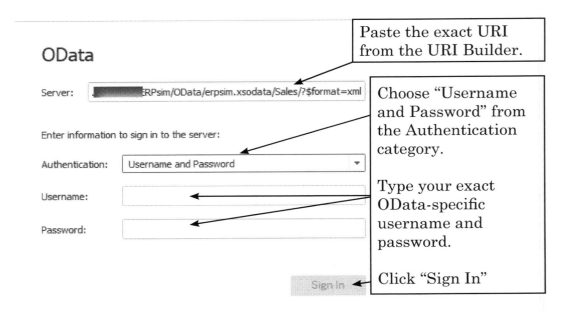

Server: [REDACTED]RPsim/OData/erpsim.xsodata/Sales/?$format=xml

> Paste the exact URI from the URI Builder.

Enter information to sign in to the server:

Authentication: Username and Password

> Choose "Username and Password" from the Authentication category.

Username:

Password:

> Type your exact OData-specific username and password.

Sign In

> Click "Sign In"

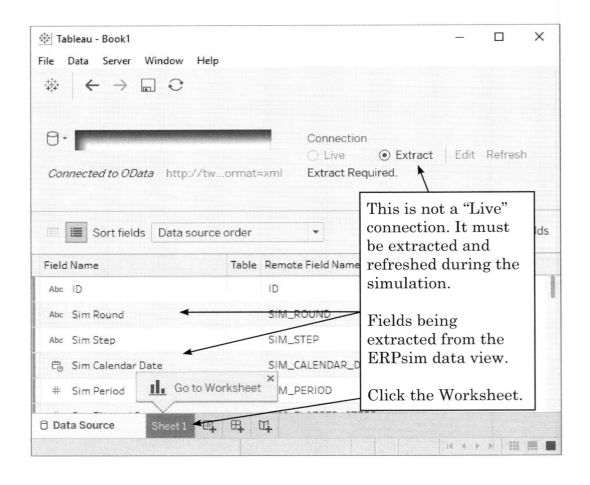

> This is not a "Live" connection. It must be extracted and refreshed during the simulation.
>
> Fields being extracted from the ERPsim data view.
>
> Click the Worksheet.

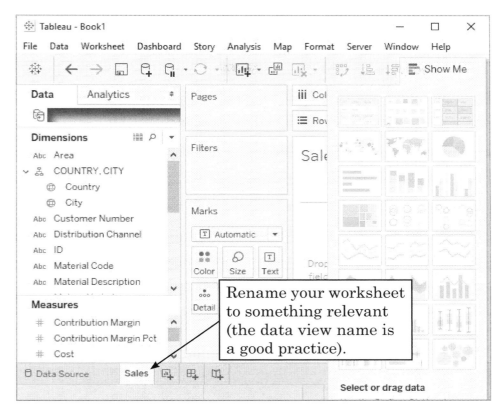

Rename your worksheet to something relevant (the data view name is a good practice).

No clue what to do in Tableau?

This textbook includes a fairly easy Tableau ERPsim data visualization using OData. Unfortunately, teaching the basics of Tableau and descriptive analytics is outside the scope of this textbook.

The instructions presume general understanding of descriptive analytics. If you have software questions, look online or ask your instructor. There are many other resources available for learning this software!

OData Connectivity Issues!

These connection instructions are fairly general. Actually connecting to and utilizing OData (especially across multiple simulations) can be far more difficult. The following are two of the most common issues with OData connectivity.

Confirm your URI!

If you did not visit the URI Builder website and create a URI specific to your ERPsim server, you will not connect to OData. Visit the URI Builder website, log in, and create the URI required for your analytics software. Go back to the start of this section for instructions on creating the URI for use with your analytics software.

Authorization Issues / Wrong Company Data

If you are receiving an error before or after you have created your OData connection, confirm your User ID and password. Remember that these OData connections require an OData-specific username and password. This will have been provided to you by your instructor or from within SAP Fiori.

To confirm or change usernames and passwords from an existing data source, locate the "data source settings" option. From within MS Excel:

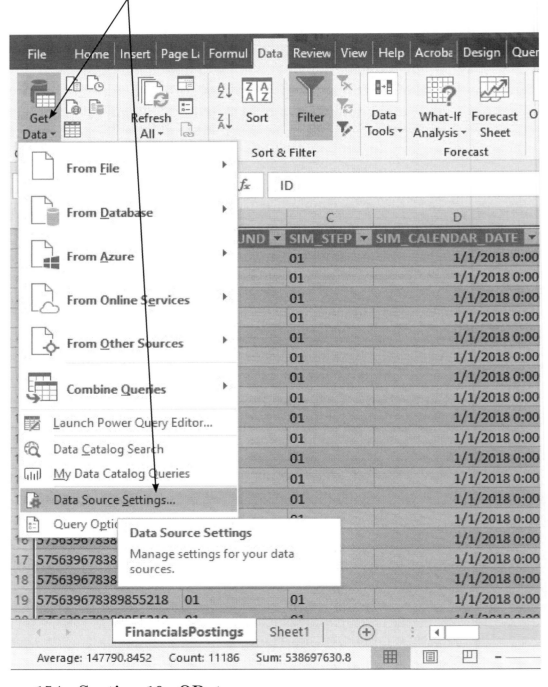

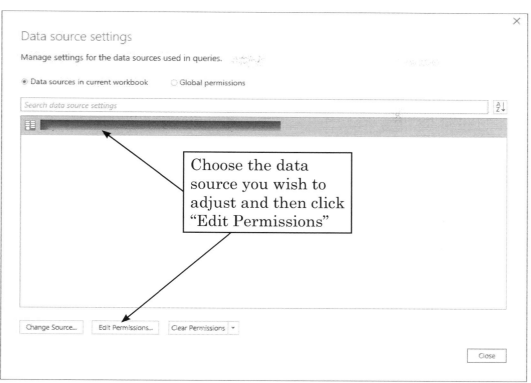

Choose the data source you wish to adjust and then click "Edit Permissions"

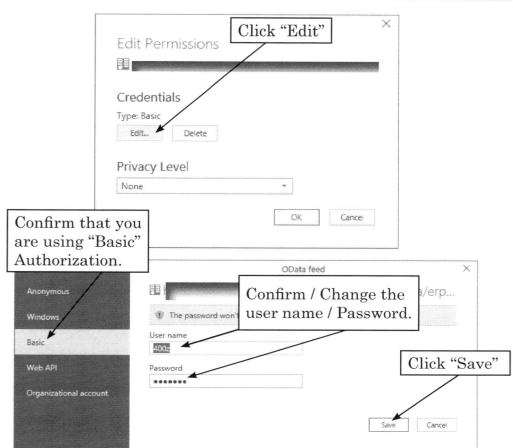

Click "Edit"

Confirm that you are using "Basic" Authorization.

Confirm / Change the user name / Password.

Click "Save"

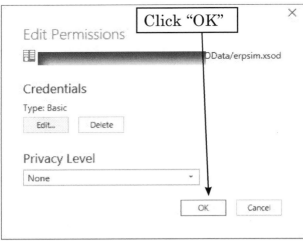

Not Using MS Excel? Issues Not Addressed Here?

You'll need to improvise. Google it, ask your instructor, click on "Help", check the ERPsim Learning Portal for your software, etc. Improvise!

Most issues with OData connectivity come from either using the incorrect URI, or authorization issues. If confirming the URI and username / password doesn't solve your issue... improvise!

OData Company Valuation

In that your team's rank is based on your Company Valuation, it's a good idea to have a real-time Company Valuation calculation handy. What better way to do this than OData?!?

These Instructions Presume That:

- You've read the strategy section on "Company Valuation"
- You have some familiarity with accounting (debits / credits) and GL Accounts
- You have at least one round of ERPsim data (and the simulation is paused)
    - You have the current calculated company valuation from the viewer
- You've made the connection to the URI Builder (see section on "OData")
- You have some familiarity with spreadsheet data modeling
- You have downloaded the MS Excel "ERPsim OData" template from www.TheCourseWebsite.com

If you are missing any of the above, work through those requirements and then come back to this point.

Using OData to Calculate Company Valuation

Before we can calculate anything, we need to acquire your team's ERPsim data. Do realize that exactly zero of the screen shots, numbers, and calculations will match your team's unique data points. The screen shots are not meant to be taken literally.

Because we will be using MS Excel, the basic ERPsim data view from the URI Builder will work for us.

> There are numerous versions and configurations of MS Excel, so you may need to improvise. Look online, click "Help", etc. The following screenshots are from Excel Office365 Version 1808.
>
> If you are stuck, contact your instructor (or Google it!).

From within the "ERPsim OData" spreadsheet (downloaded from this textbook's website, www.TheCourseWebsite.com), create a new data connection.

Follow the connection instructions from within the previous "OData" section.

When prompted to choose your data view, choose "FinancialsPostings".

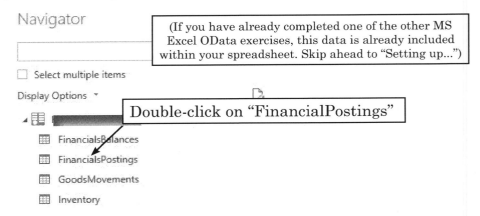

Load the data into any blank worksheet. Rename that worksheet to "FinancialsPostings".

Inspect the Financial Data

This data view is, quite literally, all of the relevant values from your ERPsim company's general ledger account. You can do quite a bit with this data.

For more information regarding what is included within this and other data views, read through the ERPsim "Reference Guide" from the ERPsim Learning Portal. (See the OData section for more details).

The ERPsim Participant's Guide gives a more detailed explanation of the GL accounts included within this report. We are only interested in the accounts relevant to creating a company valuation calculator.

Setting Up The Spreadsheet

The first step within the Company Valuation calculation is calculating "Debt Load". This calculation takes the current debts, subtracts short-term assets, and assesses how much debt is remaining.

To calculate each GL account value within our spreadsheet, we'll use the SUMIF function. We'll "SUM" the GL value "IF" the GL account is present within that data row.

Click to the "Company Valuation" tab within the Excel document.

Within cell B4, type the SUMIF function:

=SUMIF(FinancialsPostings!H:H,"0000113101",FinancialsPostings!R:R)

Within cell B5, type the SUMIF function:

=SUMIF(FinancialsPostings!H:H,"0000160000",FinancialsPostings!R:R)

Within cell B6, type the SUMIF function:

=SUMIF(FinancialsPostings!H:H,"0000113300",FinancialsPostings!R:R)

Within cell B7, type the SUMIF function:

=SUMIF(FinancialsPostings!H:H,"0000140000",FinancialsPostings!R:R)

> It is outside the scope of this textbook to teach general accounting and Excel functionality. If you aren't sure why what you're doing is coming back with the values you're receiving, Google it or ask your instructor.

At this point you should have four values for each GL item. You can confirm that these calculations have completed accurately by comparing them to F.01:

Financial Statement Item/Account	Tot.Rpt.Pr
Balance Sheet	0.00
Assets	28,555,943.06
Current assets	1,769,276.38
113300 Bank Cash Account	733,271.62
00 Customers - Domestic Receiva	1,036,004.76
m assets	26,786,666.68
d Owners' Equity	28,555,943.06-
	8,438,798.00-
nt liabilities	8,438,798.00-
3101 Bank Loan	8,000,000.00-
160000 Accounts payable-domestic	438,798.00-

GL Account	Values
Bank Loan	8,000,000.00
Accounts Payable	438,798.00
Cash	(733,271.62)
Accounts Receivables	(1,036,004.76)

If your calculations do not match, retrace your steps. Excel requires exact information to function properly. Did you type a GL account incorrectly? Is the function typed correctly?

> Keep in mind that these instructions are based on the 2019-2020 release of the ERPsim Manufacturing Game. If you are utilizing an outdated copy of this textbook, these steps may have changed.
> **Contact Your Instructor for Assistance!**

Calculate Your Debt Load and Risk Rate

Within cell B9 type =SUM(B4:B7)

This will calculate your Debt Load:

	A	B	C
B9		=SUM(B4:B7)	
1	**Company Valuation**		
2			
3	GL Account	Values	
4	Bank Loan	8,000,000.00	
5	Accounts Payable	438,798.00	
6	Cash	(733,271.62)	
7	Accounts Receivables	(1,036,004.76)	
8			
9	Debt Load	€ 6,669,521.62	

To calculate your company's risk rate, add the following VLOOKUP() function into cell B12:

=VLOOKUP(B9,'Net Debt Table'!A3:D23,4)

This looks up your Risk Differential within the "Net Debt Table" tab.

Calculate your Risk Rate. Within cell B13 type =B11+B12

With your Debt Load calculated you should now have your Risk Rate:

	A	B
1	**Company Valuation**	
2		
3	GL Account	Values
4	Bank Loan	8,000,000.00
5	Accounts Payable	438,798.00
6	Cash	(733,271.62)
7	Accounts Receivables	(1,036,004.76)
8		
9	Debt Load	€ 6,669,521.62
10		
11	Market Risk	7.00%
12	Risk Differential	5.25%
13	Risk Rate	12.25%

Rounds Completed. Manual or automatic?

The easy option for Rounds Completed is for you to just type the number of rounds completed. Keep in mind that the eventual Company Valuation calculation is only accurate between rounds with the simulation paused.

If you intend to manually update this calculation, type the number of rounds completed within cell B15.

If you would like to automatically calculate the number of rounds completed... within cell B15 type =(MAX(FinancialsPostings!F:F)-1)/20

> Remember that explanation for each ERPsim field, its meaning, and purpose can be found within the ERPsim Reference Guide. Explanations of GL accounts (and more!) can be found within the ERPsim Participant's Guide. (Or... ask your instructor!)

If you choose to automatically calculate "Rounds Completed", this can be refreshed to update as the simulation is running. Do note that it is only accurate between rounds with the simulation paused. Be sure to confirm your calculated Company Valuation between rounds!

Net Income and Revised Net Income

Within cell B16 type:

=SUMIF(FinancialsPostings!J:J,"Income Statement",FinancialsPostings!R:R)

Because an investment in Setup Time Reduction adjusts the Company Valuation calculation, we need to calculate your team's total Setup Time Reduction.

Within cell B17 type:

=SUMIF(FinancialsPostings!H:H,"0000478000",FinancialsPostings!R:R)

Within cell B18 type =B16+B17

From your financial statement confirm your calculated net income and investment in setup time reduction (lean manufacturing):

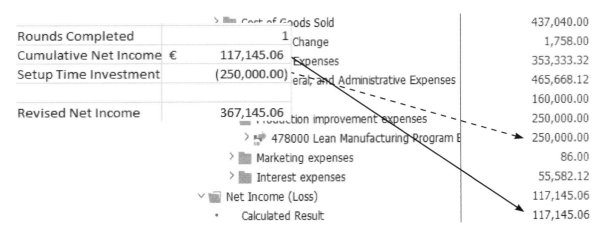

			Cost of Goods Sold	437,040.00
Rounds Completed		1	Change	1,758.00
Cumulative Net Income €	117,145.06	Expenses	353,333.32
Setup Time Investment	(250,000.00)	eral, and Administrative Expenses	465,668.12
			160,000.00
Revised Net Income	367,145.06	tion improvement expenses	250,000.00
		> 478000 Lean Manufacturing Program E	250,000.00
		> Marketing expenses	86.00
		> Interest expenses	55,582.12
		Net Income (Loss)	117,145.06
		Calculated Result	117,145.06

Annualized Net Income and Company Valuation

At this point you have calculated your company's debt load, risk rate, and revised net income. The final company valuation calculation requires an annualized net income. ERPsim is programmed for 12 rounds, though, most courses only complete a few 20-day rounds. How do we annualize net income?

This is where the "Rounds Completed" calculation comes into play. We have to estimate annual net income, 12 rounds of ERPsim, from our revised Net Income.

Luckily, this is an easy calculation within Excel.

Within cell B21 type =(B19/(B15/12))+B17

This calculation takes your revised net income and divides it by the remaining rounds (rounds completed divided by 12). It then adds any setup time investments to the annual net income. (Note that setup time reduction is a negative value. You are "subtracting" setup time from the annualized net income.)

At this point, you have everything you need for to calculate your valuation.

Within cell B23 type =B21/B13

Compare your calculated company valuation with the ERPsim viewer's result.

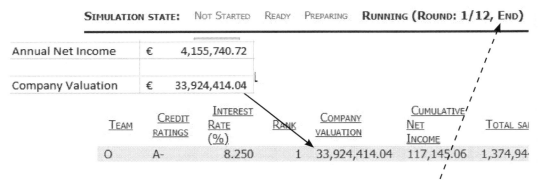

If your numbers don't match, retrace your steps. This final calculation is based on several previous numbers, all of which can be confirmed within your financial statements. Try calculating this without OData. Where are the numbers incorrect? Can't figure it out? Contact your instructor!

> This calculation is only accurate between rounds (with the simulation paused). If the simulation is actively running, you have no way to confirm that your company valuation is accurate. Wait until the simulation is paused between rounds and then compare.

OData and Production

Effective and efficient production is the foundation to a winning ERPsim strategy! Why? Without production, there can't be any revenue. And without revenue, expenses continue to accrue. The end result is negative net income.

These Instructions Presume That:

- You've read through the sections on ERPsim Strategy
- You have some familiarity with accounting (debits / credits) and GL Accounts
- You have at least one round of ERPsim data (and the simulation is paused)
- You've made the connection to the URI Builder (see section on "OData")
- You have some familiarity with spreadsheet data modeling
- You have downloaded the MS Excel "ERPsim OData" template from www.TheCourseWebsite.com

If you are missing any of the above, work through those requirements and then come back to this point.

Using OData to Calculate Production Estimates!

Before we can calculate anything, we need to acquire your team's ERPsim data. Do realize that exactly zero of the screen shots, numbers, and calculations will match your team's unique data points. The screen shots are not meant to be taken literally.

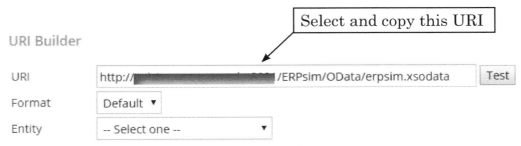

Because we will be using MS Excel, the basic ERPsim data view from the URI Builder will work for us.

> There are numerous versions and configurations of MS Excel, so you may need to improvise. Look online, click "Help", etc. The following screenshots are from Excel Office 365 Version 1808.
>
> If you are stuck, contact your instructor (or Google it!).

From within the "ERPsim OData" spreadsheet (downloaded from this textbook's website, www.TheCourseWebsite.com), create a new data connection.

Follow the connection instructions from within the previous "OData" section.

When prompted to choose your data view, choose "FinancialsPostings".

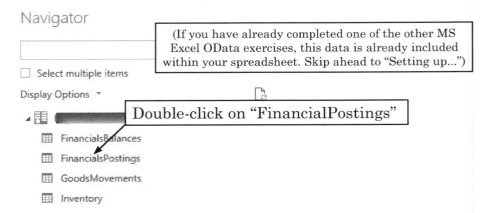

Load the data into any blank worksheet. Rename that worksheet to "FinancialsPostings".

Inspect the Financial Data

This data view is, quite literally, all of the relevant values from your ERPsim company's general ledger. You can do quite a bit with this data.

> For more information regarding what is included within this and other data views, read through the ERPsim "Reference Guide" from the ERPsim Learning Portal. (See the OData section for more details).

The ERPsim Participant's Guide gives a more detailed explanation of the GL accounts included within this report. We are only interested in the accounts relevant to creating a production estimate calculator.

Setting Up The Spreadsheet

The first step within the OData production estimate is to use accounting data to calculate your production capacity and the remaining days of production.

To calculate, we'll use GL account values from within our spreadsheet. We'll use the SUMIF function; we'll "SUM" the GL value "IF" the GL account is present within that data row.

Click to the "Production Estimate" tab within the Excel document.

Within cell B4, type the SUMIF function:

=SUMIF(FinancialsPostings!H:H,"0000011000",FinancialsPostings!Q:Q)

Within cell B5, type the SUMIF function:

=SUMIF(FinancialsPostings!J:J,"Income Statement",FinancialsPostings!R:R)

Within cell B6, type the SUMIF function:

=(MAX(FinancialsPostings!F:F)-1)

> It is outside the scope of this textbook to teach general accounting and Excel functionality. If you aren't sure why what you're doing is coming back with the values you're receiving, Google it or ask your instructor.

At this point you should have three values for each listed GL item.

You can confirm that the Machinery and Equipment calculation has completed accurately by comparing it to F.01:

Financial Statement Item/Account	Tot.Rpt.Pr
Balance Sheet	0.00
Assets	28,555,943.06
Current assets	1,769,276.38
term assets	26,786,666.68
250000001000 Land	500,000.00
2000 Buildings	1,500,000.00
202010 Accumulated Depreciation - B	5,000.00-
011000 Machinery and equipment	25,000,000.00
011010 Accumulated depreciation - m	208,333.32-

GL Account Balances	
Machinery and equip.	
Net Income	€ 117,145.06
Days Completed	20

Confirm your Net Income and Days Completed calculations in the ERPsim Viewer.

SIMULATION STATE: NOT STARTED   READY   PREPARING   **RUNNING (ROUND: 1/12, END)**

ADMIN BANKER VIEWER RESULTS

FINANCIAL STATEMENTS - R1

TEAM	CREDIT RATINGS	INTEREST RATE (%)	RANK	COMPANY VALUATION	CUMULATIVE NET INCOME	TOTAL SAl
O	A-	8.250	1	33,924,414.04	117,145.06	1,374,94

If your calculations do not match, retrace your steps. Excel requires exact information to function properly. Did you type a GL account incorrectly? Is the function typed correctly?

Adjust Inputs as Necessary

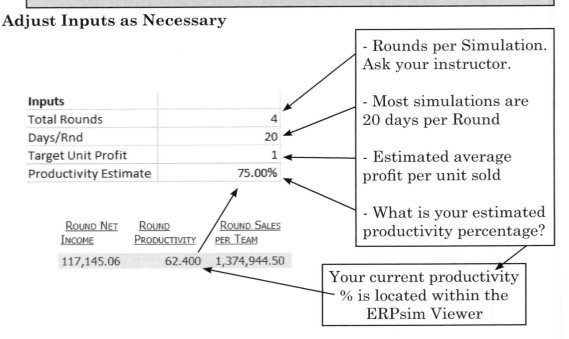

- Rounds per Simulation. Ask your instructor.

- Most simulations are 20 days per Round

- Estimated average profit per unit sold

- What is your estimated productivity percentage?

Your current productivity % is located within the ERPsim Viewer

Inputs

Total Rounds	4
Days/Rnd	20
Target Unit Profit	1
Productivity Estimate	75.00%

ROUND NET INCOME	ROUND PRODUCTIVITY	ROUND SALES PER TEAM
117,145.06	62.400	1,374,944.50

Estimated Remaining Production

Based on your GL Account balances and the above inputs, the spreadsheet will automatically calculate your estimated remaining production and estimated net income. How is this calculated? If you look at each calculation's formulas you'll be able to see how the GL Account Balances and inputs interrelate.

Here's a quick overview:

Machinery and equip.	€	25,000,000	Daily Capacity	25000

For each million invested in Machinery and Equipment, you will have 1,000 in daily capacity. You start the simulation with 24,000,000 euro's worth of Machinery and Equipment, or, 24,000 in daily capacity.

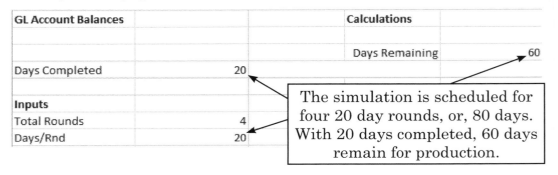

GL Account Balances		Calculations	
		Days Remaining	60
Days Completed	20		
Inputs			
Total Rounds	4		
Days/Rnd	20		

The simulation is scheduled for four 20 day rounds, or, 80 days. With 20 days completed, 60 days remain for production.

Calculations	
Daily Capacity	25000
Days Remaining	60
Total Possible Capacity	1500000

Having a daily capacity of 25,000 units, and, 60 days remaining, the total possible capacity is 1,500,000 units.

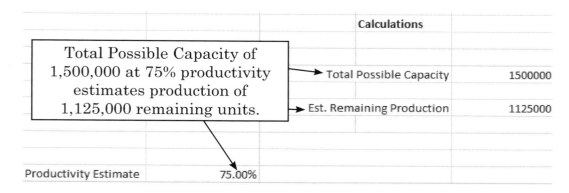

		Calculations	
Total Possible Capacity of 1,500,000 at 75% productivity estimates production of 1,125,000 remaining units.	→	Total Possible Capacity	1500000
	→	Est. Remaining Production	1125000
Productivity Estimate	75.00%		

Estimating profit of 1 euro per unit sold and 1,125,000 units of possible capacity remaining, our estimated profit / net income of €1,125,000.

Inputs		Est. Remaining Production	1125000
		Estimated Net Income	
Target Unit Profit	1	Est. Profit Remaining	1125000

Add this estimated profit to your current net income for Total Estimated Net Income:

GL Account Balances			
Net Income	€ 117,145.06		
		Estimated Net Income	
		Est. Profit Remaining	1125000
		Total Est. Net Income	€ 1,242,145.06

This completed OData spreadsheet is by no means and exhaustive look at all of the various options within ERPsim. If you haven't already, read through the various strategy sections of this textbook. There's more to it! But, this is a good start for both setting up production-related OData connectivity and estimating profit based on your productivity.

"What If?" Scenarios!

A good spreadsheet data model can help you with decision making. As noted, this is not an exhaustive look at your production, but, it is a start for determining what could happen within your production.

The easiest place to start is with your productivity estimate.

Included within this template is a simple data table which can show you estimates of various productivity percentages. It's already set to calculate productivity from 50% to 100%:

	What if? Scenario.	
	€	1,242,145.06
50%	€	867,145.06
60%	€	1,017,145.06
70%	€	1,167,145.06
80%	€	1,317,145.06
90%	€	1,467,145.06
100%	€	1,617,145.06

As noted within the sections on strategy, your productivity percentage can play a huge role in your company's profitability.

As you expand this spreadsheet, what else can you calculate?

- Investments in setup time reduction or capacity?
- The sizes of production orders you approve?
- Capacity investments versus warehouse capacity costs?
- The impact of any of the above on your company valuation?

All of the above calculations and What If? scenarios can be derived from the GL account data already included within this spreadsheet. What about the other data views? What else can you do?

Remember, all of your ERPsim strategies must be quantified or otherwise qualified. Work through these calculations between games and utilize them in "Real time" within the next simulation.

Your profitability and company valuation (and rank!) will improve!

OData and Sales

Each time the simulation is started, market preferences are reset; there is a new set of preferred products within each region. Which product is selling best and where? How do you quickly determine what you should produce to earn the most profit?

These Instructions Presume That:

- You have at least one round of ERPsim sales data
- You have some familiarity with ERPsim sales and product preferences
- You've made the connection to the URI Builder (see section on "OData")
- You have some familiarity with descriptive analytics
- Your installation of Tableau is complete and operational

If you are missing any of the above, work through those requirements and then come back to this point.

Using OData to Visualize Sales Data

Before we can calculate anything, we need to acquire your team's ERPsim data. Do realize that exactly zero of the screen shots, numbers, and visualizations will match your team's unique data points. The screen shots are not meant to be taken literally.

Because we will be using Tableau, you will need to create your ERPsim data view from within the URI Builder.

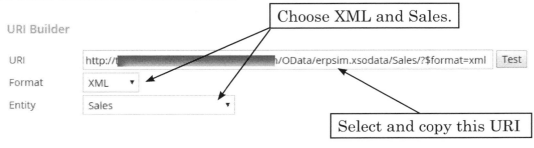

There are numerous versions and configurations of Tableau, so you may need to improvise. Look online, click "Help", etc. The following screenshots are from Tableau Desktop Professional Edition, 2019.1.3 64 bit running on the 64 bit version of Windows 10 Pro, Build 1803.

If you are stuck, contact your instructor (or Google it!).

Follow the connection instructions from within the previous "OData" section to create a connection to the above "Sales" data view.

The beauty of Tableau is that it is very easy to use. With this sales data view, you can't go wrong. Keep clicking until you see something useful! (you can't break it!)

> For more information regarding what is included within this and other data views, read through the ERPsim "Reference Guide" from the ERPsim Learning Portal. (See the OData section for more details).

Sales Per Distribution Channel

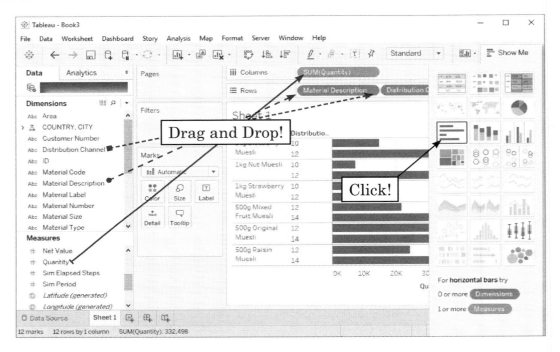

It's that easy! Compared with the tabular sales reports that are standard for ERPsim, this is very easy to interpret. Which is the top seller?

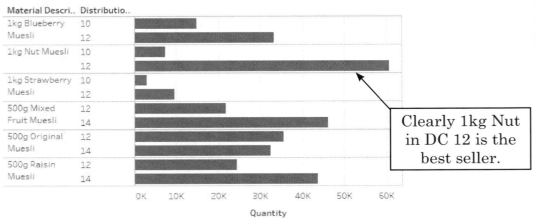

Clearly 1kg Nut in DC 12 is the best seller.

If you're using this during the simulation, remember that you have to click "refresh" to update the data. There are many ways to do this depending on where you are within Tableau. The consistent option is to click Data in the file menu and click "Refresh All Extracts":

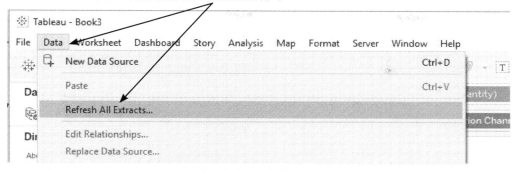

Don't be afraid to "click around" within Tableau. You really can't break it.

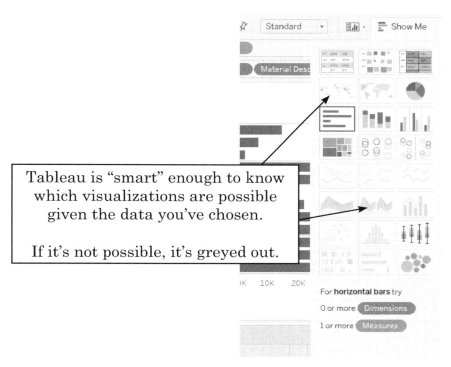

Tableau is "smart" enough to know which visualizations are possible given the data you've chosen.

If it's not possible, it's greyed out.

Tableau is Data Visualization / Descriptive Analytics

Tableau is great at organizing and showing you data—even if you aren't familiar with it already! As you click through the data, realize that you can adjust colors, sort data, filter data, and delete views you've added. Even better, find something you like but it's not quite right? Try changing the view a bit by switching the rows and columns!

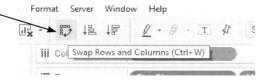

Daily Sales Data

Drag and drop these dimensions and measures:

Click!

This data view shows daily sales sorted by simulated day. During round 1 it can tell us something about the production schedule and inventory levels.

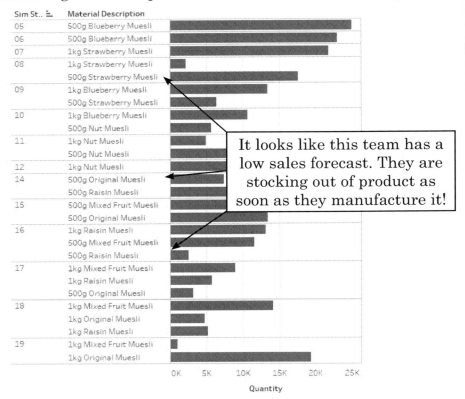

> It looks like this team has a low sales forecast. They are stocking out of product as soon as they manufacture it!

A look at the production schedule confirms it!

Order	Material description	Start	Finish	Setup	Released	Target	Confirmed	Unit Cost
1000132	1kg Original Muesli	01/17	01/18	5.00	01/06	24,000	24,000	0.00
1000134	1kg Mixed Fruit Muesli	01/16	01/17	5.00		24,000	24,000	0.00
1000126	1kg Raisin Muesli	01/15	01/16	5.00		24,000	24,000	0.00
1000125	500g Mixed Fruit Muesli	01/14	01/15	5.00		24,000	24,000	0.00
1000124	500g Original Muesli	01/13	01/14	5.00	01/05	24,000	24,000	0.00
1000121	500g Raisin Muesli	01/11	01/12	5.00		24,000	24,000	0.00
1000120	1kg Nut Muesli	01/10	01/11	5.00		24,000	24,000	0.00
1000119	500g Nut Muesli	01/09	01/10	5.00		24,000	24,000	0.00
1000118	1kg Blueberry Muesli	01/08	01/09	5.00		24,000	24,000	0.00
1000117	500g Strawberry Muesli	01/07	01/08	5.00		24,000	24,000	0.00
1000110	1kg Strawberry Muesli	01/06	01/07	5.00	01/04	24,000	24,000	0.00
1000104	500g Blueberry Muesli	01/04	01/05			48,000	48,000	0.00

When quantity was listed as the "Sum" for the entire round, it wasn't as obvious that there's a production issue. Once it is broken down by day it's easier to see that something's not right.

This would be the time for the person in charge of sales reports to give some feedback to the person in charge of production planning. Clearly the forecast is too low. There's also an argument to be made regarding the manufacture of all 12 products. Is this the best use of your production capacity?

Visualized Market Report

Close this worksheet. Go back to the URI Builder and create a URI for the "Market" data view:

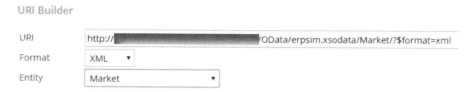

Copy and paste the URI into the OData "Server" prompt as you did for the "Sales" data view. (See OData section for a reminder on how to do this.)

Drag and drop these dimensions and measures:

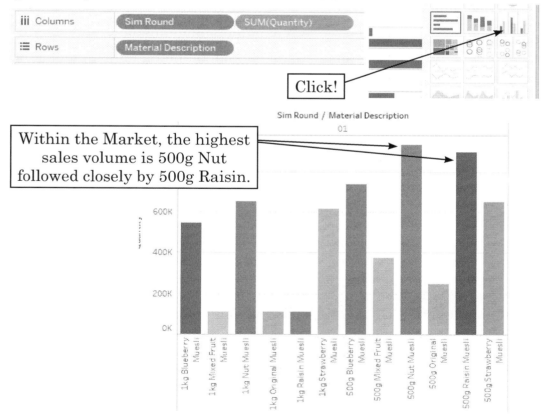

Data Views in Tableau

It's fairly "easy" to get something useful out of Tableau. Explore all of the data views. Some are better for visualizations than others.

> For more information regarding what is included within each ERPsim data view, read through the ERPsim "Reference Guide" from the ERPsim Learning Portal. (See the OData section for more details).

Adjusting the Data in Tableau

Some of the data that Tableau processes can be adjusted so that it is more useful. It's outside the scope of this textbook to make those adjustments. However, those calculations and adjustments can be seen for each Dimension / Measure by clicking the down arrow on any Dimension / Measure.

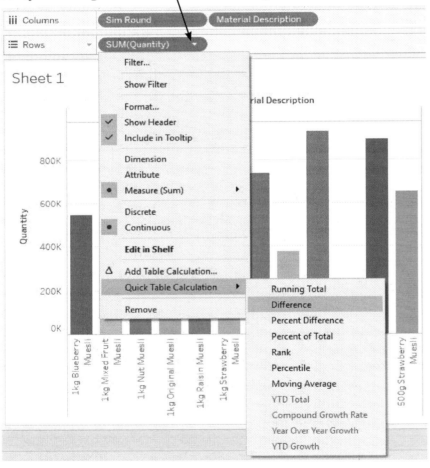

For more information on what you can do with Tableau, Google it, click "help", read through the Tableau specific information in the ERPsim Learning Portal, or ... just click around! If you have an idea of what the data is, Tableau can be fairly simple to navigate.

Part V

ERPsim Extras!

Section 11 - SAP Fiori

As noted at the start of this textbook, the SAP ECC to S/4 Migration will be taking place over the next several years. If your instructor is including this migration within your course, this section will help introduce the SAP Fiori interface for ERPsim.

To better understand SAP Fiori, let's start with the SAP GUI.

Using the SAP GUI with SAP ERP

For over two decades, the SAP GUI has been most end users' only interface with the SAP ERP system. While it has changed in look and function over the years, to many, it hasn't change all that much.

The SAP GUI transactions, T-Codes, are designed by SAP to follow "best practice" processes and to meet the needs of many different types of organizations and end users.

To many, the screens are "busy" and for those wanting to streamline the end user experience, customization is at best difficult and at worst a disaster. (Google it! There are many case studies regarding SAP T-Code customization!)

With a complete redesign of the structure and code behind the new SAP ERP, S/4 HANA, a new user interface is available: SAP Fiori

What is SAP Fiori?

Fiori is just an interface. It's not a new module within the ERP system, it's not a server, a data protocol, or anything but a way to interface with the ERP system. Compared with the SAP GUI, which is an application installed on Windows / Mac, Fiori is a web application. Any modern and up-to-date web browser can be used to access the S/4 HANA ERP system.

This "web application" descriptor is important as modern web browsers are visual in nature, and, offer quite a bit of flexibility and customization. The options with SAP Fiori are nearly unlimited in the data it can access. SAP Fiori, as an interface with the SAP S/4 HANA ERP system, has many options not possible with the traditional SAP GUI. Customization is encouraged. Visualizations are "built in". It's all about the user experience (UX), meaning, the end user only needs to see what they need to see. No more SAP transaction customization!

SAP Fiori Customization: Two Examples using ERPsim

If you've been using the SAP GUI with ERPsim, you have likely been exposed to either the production process or changing prices.

The ERPsim Production Process

From the ERPsim job aid:

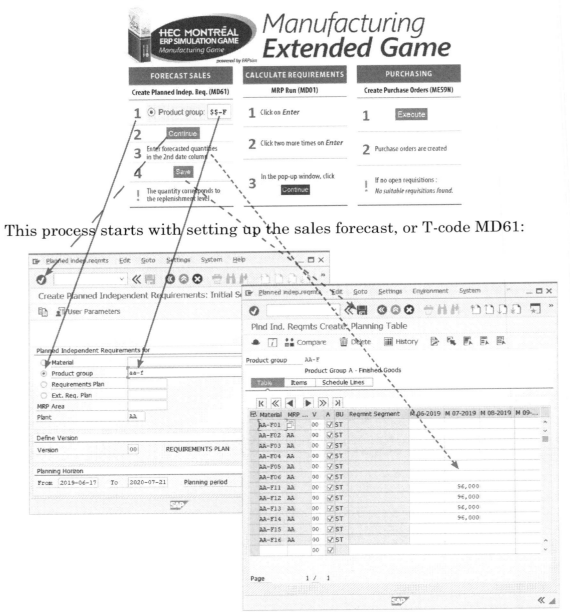

This process starts with setting up the sales forecast, or T-code MD61:

Once the forecast is saved, you must execute MRP.

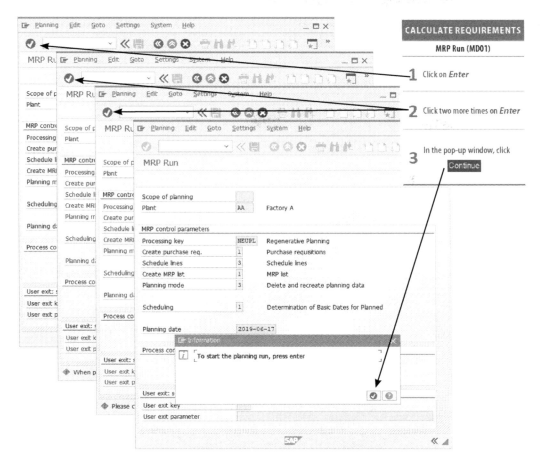

Followed by a report which has little meaning to the average ERPsim user:

Thinking through this process from an end-user experience, there are MANY options within each transaction. Within MD61, the selection screen, typing the information within column 2, clicking save. Then, opening transaction MD01, looking at ALL of those options, clicking enter, enter, enter...

As an end user, what do you actually need to see?

The following is Baton Simulation's SAP Fiori interpretation of this same part of the ERPsim production process:

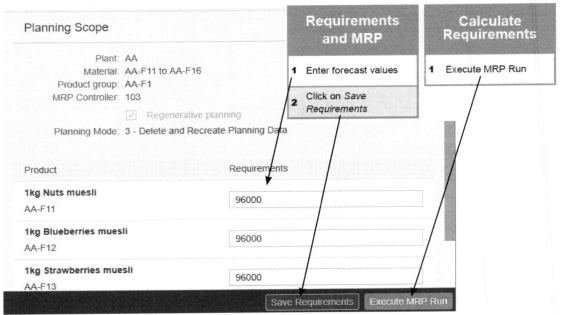

Realizing that there is no need for the typical ERPsim end user to "click through" two transactions, selection screens, and options and parameters, this part of the process is reduced to one screen and a few options.

For this particular customization, both transactions have been reduced to one "app" within the Fiori dashboard. Only what's necessary is shown, and, there's no need to move between multiple transactions.

From a process perspective, for this particular end user, nothing "internal" has changed. The same ERP system is behind all of this. And, the SAP GUI will show the same results. But, why would you continue to use the SAP GUI if the process can be reduced to a few text boxes and buttons within one transaction?

Changing Prices in ERPsim

If you've been part of changing prices within ERPsim, you know that it is a multi-step process. You also, probably, have multiple screens open: sales reports, inventory levels, maybe some sort of analytics? You're constantly looking between various SAP GUI transactions / reports making a decision on which product's price to change within each distribution channel.

For this example, we'll focus on changing prices within the SAP GUI:

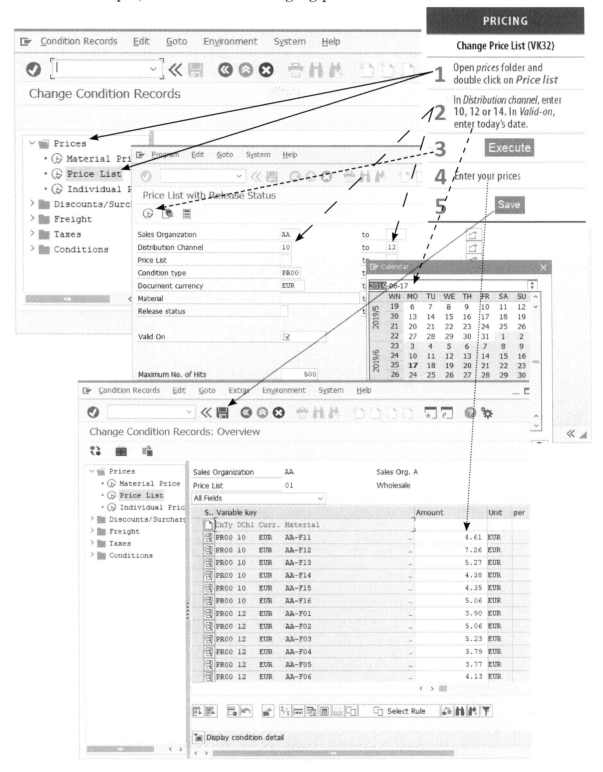

Thinking through this process from an end-user experience, there are MANY options within this one transaction. There is so much information that needs to be entered, and, the "enter price" screen requires scrolling through multiple levels of product listings per distribution channel.

Keep in mind that the person making these changes also has multiple screens open checking sales reports, inventory, and costs.

The question becomes: As an end user, what do you actually need to see?

The following is Baton Simulation's SAP Fiori interpretation of price changes:

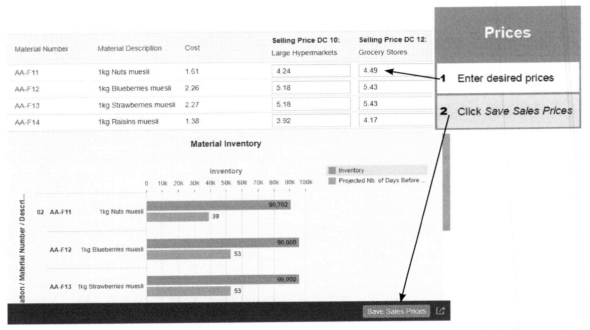

In addition to making it easier to change prices, the typical information necessary to make a pricing decision is included!

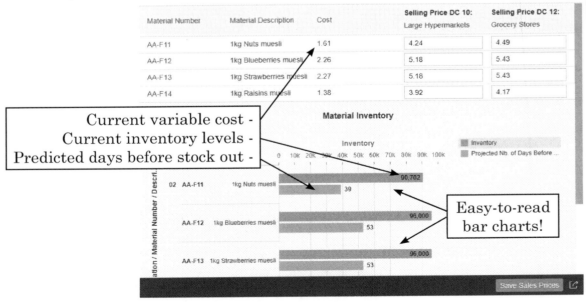

Realizing that there is no need for the typical ERPsim end user to "click through" multiple selection screens, options, and parameters all while viewing multiple rerports... this part of the process is reduced to one screen and a few options.

For this particular customization, one transaction and multiple reports have been reduced to one "app" within the Fiori dashboard. Only what's necessary is shown, and, there's no need to move between multiple screens and reports.

From a process perspective, for this particular end user, nothing "internal" has changed. The same ERP system is behind all of this. And, the SAP GUI will show the same results. But, why use the SAP GUI if the process can be reduced to a few text boxes, reports, and buttons within one transaction?

What Else Can you do with SAP Fiori?

While streamlining processes is a great use of this new SAP interface, there is so much more that is possible. Because Fiori is web-based, anything you can do on the web can be integrated into the interface!

Baton Simulations, the commercial side of ERPsim, also offers DAS, Digital Adoption Solution, to aid with web-based organizational learning. While it is most often associated with SAP Fiori, it can be implemented with any web-based platform.

Because this textbook focuses on ERPsim, we'll focus on how DAS can be implemented for ERPsim.

Training is Built In!

Remember those first days as you were learning ERPsim? There are so many different options and parameters to consider. Plus, navigating SAP, reading reports, making decisions?

This isn't any different in the "Real World". Whether an organization is using SAP, IFS ERP, Epicor, or any other ERP system, a user's first days with the ERP system can be challenging. How do you balance the right amount of training with documentation and expecting the end user to ask questions as necessary? What if you could just build all of it right into the ERP system?

Using Baton Simulation's DAS with ERPsim, not only can you have that training right there, it can also walk you through the process explaining each step along the way. Remember those transactions you don't use that often? Or, the day a team member wasn't available and you had to perform their role? What do you do? How do you use it?

Within SAP Fiori enhanced with Baton Simulation's DAS, just right-click the tile. Don't remember how to update the sales forecast and execute MRP?

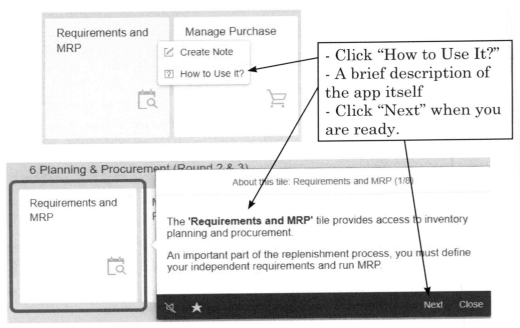

The built-in training automatically opens the tile and walks you through elements of the transaction:

The independent requirements represent the sales forecast of your finished products (boxes of cereal muesli).

The amount you decide to plan is what you wish to have right after the **replenishment and the production are successful**.

What if the Built In Training isn't Enough?

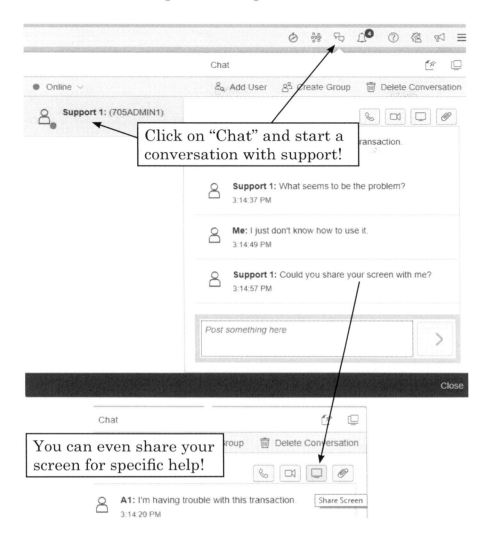

Baton Simulations' DAS is a great example for what can be done with SAP Fiori. If you can think of something you can do on the web, it can be customized into your SAP experience.

Geospatial Analytics

As an example that is not only specific to ERPsim, but, any sales manager within the "real world", where are your customers, how much do they buy, and where are your largest sales areas?

Again using Baton Simulations' interpretation of ERPsim, we can overlay sales data across a map. In this particular case we'll look at total sales per customer across all of Germany. The details will be noted by "circles", which are already programmed to enlarge based on sales quantity.

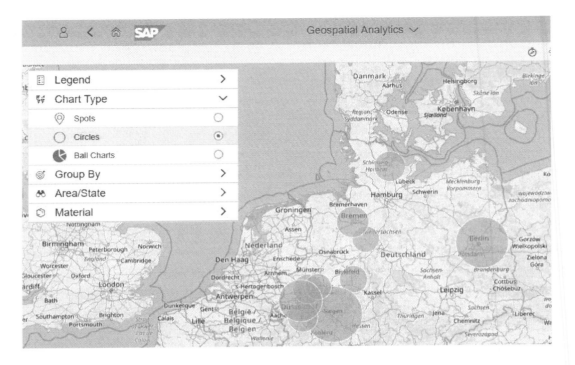

If you start thinking about your own experience with ERPsim, you may start to come up with other ideas of how this web-based interface could be configured to enhance your experience. Did you create something within OData that helps your team make decisions? You could build it in to SAP Fiori! Something outside of ERPsim that could be used with ERPsim data? You could build it in to SAP Fiori!

Academics and ERPsim

As implied, Baton Simulations' ERPsim enhancement go along with the commercial side of ERPsim. In that you are using an academically-oriented ERPsim textbook, your SAP Fiori options are not as exciting.

Why?

The original and ongoing purpose of ERPsim, especially the Manufacturing Game, is to teach students about cross-functional business processes. If the academic version of ERPsim were reduced to a few clicks with built-in analytics, how would it differ from other business simulations? Where is student discovery of strategies? Building analytics that match your team's strategies?

And, with that, how does the academic version of ERPsim look in Fiori?

The next section will walk you through ERPsim with SAP Fiori.

Section 12 - ERPsim in Fiori

If you are approaching this course starting from the SAP GUI and "migrating" to SAP Fiori, you will likely transition fairly quickly.

If you haven't already, you should read the previous section on SAP Fiori before starting this section.

SAP Fiori and ERPsim

Fiori for ERPsim follows a similar layout to the Manufacturing Game job aid. Like the job aid, Fiori is organized by function / role within the simulation. While the same person may perform multiple roles, information and tiles related to each role are grouped together.

These role groupings are part of the ERPsim home screen's header:

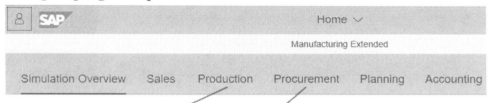

By clicking on any of the headers, you will automatically be moved to the tiles which relate to that particular ERPsim role.

Of particular interest is the built-in feedback you'll receive within each tile. You can see above that there are open purchase orders awaiting delivery. There are 6 planned orders to be converted. Without opening any of the tiles, you already have an idea of the company's current status.

Taking a look at the tiles, you'll see that the transaction code and description from the SAP GUI job aid is included:

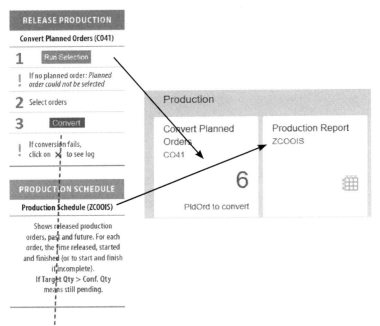

While the interface is different, most of the apps themselves look nearly identical to the SAP GUI transactions they are based off of.

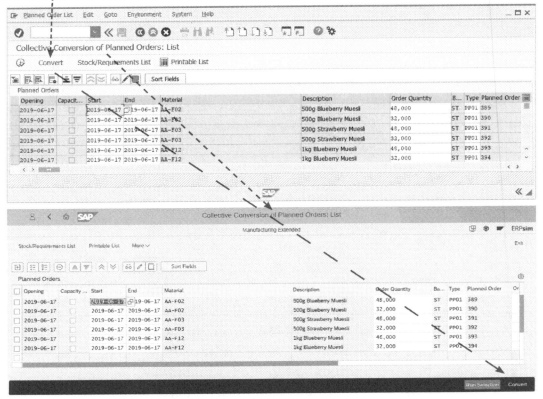

But not all reports look the same!

Fiori Visualizations!

Some of the reports look different, and, have layout options. A sales report:

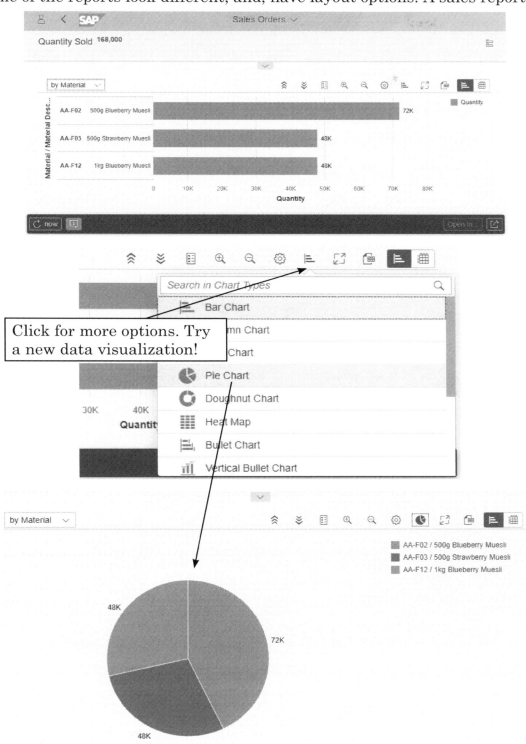

Click for more options. Try a new data visualization!

If you're already familiar with ERPsim through the SAP GUI, the best option as you get to know Fiori is to "click around". Most participant's who move from the SAP GUI to SAP Fiori feel it takes some "getting used to", but, agree that it is inherently more intuitive. Above all, the various visualization options for some of the reports makes things much easier!

Multiple Transactions at Once

Just like with the SAP GUI, you can "start a new session". This isn't as easy as pressing the "new session" button, but, it's not difficult.

From the "Home" screen:

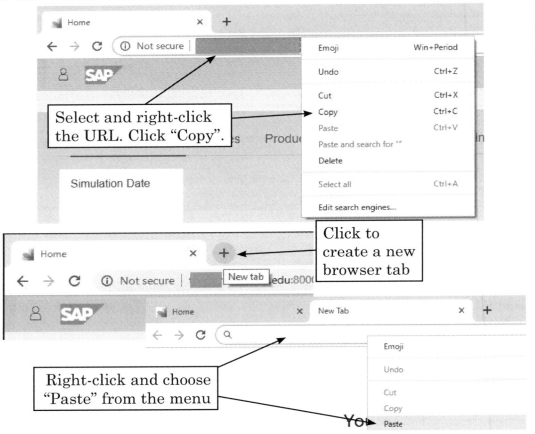

You Can Still use the SAP / Web GUI!

Not ready to go "all in" with Fiori? Ask your instructor for the SAP GUI information for your server / client. You can also use the Web GUI, which requires a special link.

Enjoy!

Section 13 - Logistics

The ERPsim Advanced Manufacturing Game is nearly the same as the Extended Manufacturing Game. As a company, you and your team are responsible for procuring raw materials, producing finished goods, utilizing reports to determine sales trends, and updating pricing and marketing accordingly. What's different? Logistics.

Within the Advanced Manufacturing Game, not only do you have to produce and sell the finished goods, you also have to figure out how those products will get to your customers.

Regions and Storage Locations

As you know from within the Extended Manufacturing Game, the German market is divided into three regions: North, South, and West. There are also three Distribution Channels (DCs): 10, 12, and 14.

Within the Advanced Manufacturing Game, your finished goods are produced and stored within a main warehouse, but each region has its own storage location—customers are not permitted to buy directly from the main warehouse, nor from a storage location outside of their geographic area.

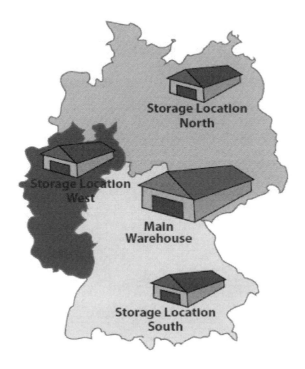

New Storage Locations

Each regional customer must purchase finished goods from a regional storage location. Each regional storage location is noted within the updated inventory report, T-Code ZMB52:

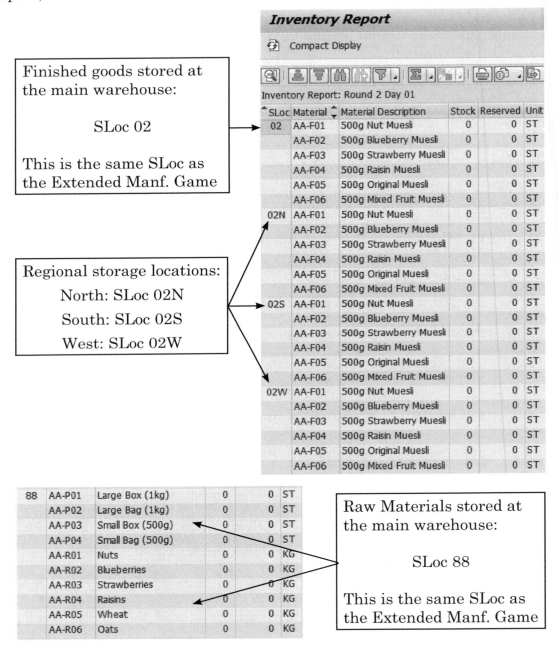

Finished goods stored at the main warehouse:

SLoc 02

This is the same SLoc as the Extended Manf. Game

Regional storage locations:
North: SLoc 02N
South: SLoc 02S
West: SLoc 02W

Raw Materials stored at the main warehouse:

SLoc 88

This is the same SLoc as the Extended Manf. Game

Customers can ONLY purchase from your regional storage locations

Warehouse Capacity

Just like within the Extended Manufacturing Game, you have warehouse capacity within your main warehouse. If you exceed your main warehouse's capacity, you are charged to rent additional space:

STORAGE CAPACITY AND COSTS		
Product type	Current space	Cost per additional 50,000 units*
Finished product	250,000 boxes	€500/day
Raw materials	250,000 kg	€1 000/day
Packaging (bags and boxes)	750,000 units	€100/day

*Billed automatically

Your regional storage space, however, is all rented space. ANY finished product you send to a regional storage location requires daily rental expenses at the rates listed above. Using the rates above, 1 finished product within a regional storage location will cost you €500 per day. Any combination of finished products within that storage location, up to 250,000 boxes, will cost €500 per day. As soon as you exceed that space, you must rent additional space. With that in mind, 250,001 finished products will require additional storage space and will cost you €1,000 per day.

Stock Transfer: T-Code ZMB1B

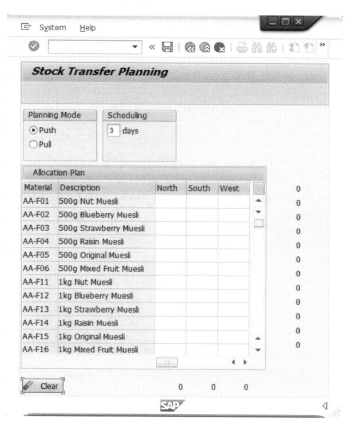

Customers can only purchase from regional storage locations, regardless of what is in stock at the main warehouse or other regional storage locations. Use transaction code ZMB1B to set your logistics strategy.

This transaction may not look all that complicated, but there are MAJOR decision points to be made. Let's look at each section of the transaction one-by-one.

Push or Pull?

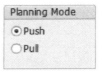

The Planning Mode covers two strategies for sending finished goods to the regional storage locations. Which strategy is best? It depends. Let's define the two strategies:

Push – At a regular interval, your main warehouse transfers a specified amount of finished goods to each of the regional storage locations. Finished goods are "pushed" to each regional storage location, regardless of the regional location's current stock level.

As an example, every 3 days the main warehouse may send 2500 finished goods to the regional storage location, regardless of the storage location's current inventory level.

Pull – At a regular interval, your main warehouse assesses the current inventory of each regional storage location and only transfers enough inventory to meet the listed stock level.

For example, every 3 days the main warehouse will assess the regional storage location's current inventory and transfer just enough finished goods to meet the specified inventory level. If the level is set for 2000, and the regional warehouse has 500, 1500 of the finished good will be sent to the regional warehouse.

How Often?

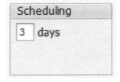

How often do you "Push" or "Pull" your finished goods to the regional storage locations?

There is no right or wrong answer. However, each time you send finished products to each location, it costs €1,000 per location. Too often and the expenses eat into your net income. Less often and you risk a stock out (remember, regional customers can only purchase from your regional storage location).

In order to determine how often you send products to your warehouse, you'll want to watch the sales reports. What's selling? How much is selling? Where is it selling? Factor in your production capacity and sales forecast—can you deliver on time?

This may seem like an easy decision, but it's not. Too often and you risk increased expenses which reduce your net income. Not often enough and you risk a stock out in a region.

Plan wisely. Quantify your decisions. Make changes as necessary.

How Many of each Finished Product to each Region?

You have twelve possible finished goods. You have three regions. How much do you push or pull to each region? This number needs to work together with your sales forecast and how much you plan to sell in each region. Remember that every time the simulation is run each geographic area has a preference for certain products. It's up to you to determine what is selling and in which region. You may sell 1,000s per day in one region, and 100s per day of the same product in another region. You'll need to watch the sales reports to determine what is selling, and how much is desired in each region.

Think About Your Capacity

With the standard capacity to produce 24,000 finished goods per day and set up time between products of 8 hours, you are limited to how much your company can produce every day. Think back to the sales forecast section...

Depending on the length of the scheduled production run, your company's daily production capacity will end up somewhere between:

$$16,000 \ (1,000 * 16 \ \text{hours}) \ \text{and} \ 24,000 \ (1,000 * 24 \ \text{hours})$$

How many finished goods can you manufacture within a day? As a "guess", consider an average of the minimum and maximum production per day:

$$\text{Minimum} = 16,000 \quad \text{Maximum} = 24,000$$

$$\text{Average} = \textbf{20,000} \ \text{finished products per 24 hour day}$$

With multiple finished goods and the required set up time, your company should expect to manufacture the average each day, 20,000.

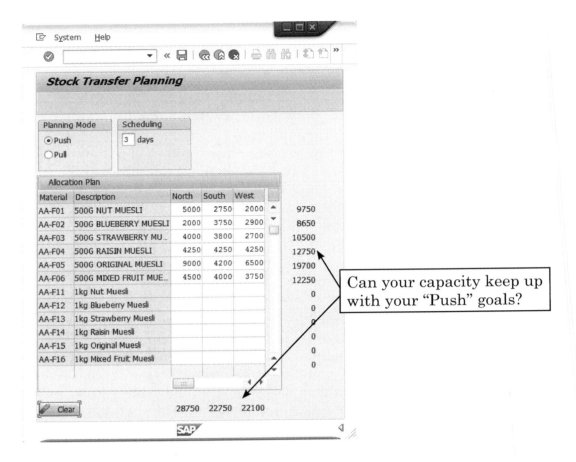

Daily Average and Scheduling

This daily average should factor into your push/pull strategy. You don't want to push more than your daily average can handle. With a daily average of 20,000, your push/pull strategy should be scheduled to match your average capacity.

Consider a strategy which is above your average daily strategy. What would happen within the following scenario?

Using the above example, your company expects to "Push" (28,750 + 22,750 + 22,100) = 73,600 finished goods every three days. Yet, your capacity and setup time states that your average three-day manufacturing capacity is 20,000 * 3 = 60,000.

Based on your company's current capacity and setup time, you should only expect to push about 60,000 every 3 days. You can't possibly meet the above "Push" strategy.

Don't Forget Your Sales Forecast!

Your sales forecast should also reflect how much you plan to "Push" or "Pull" within your scheduled stock transfer planning. If you forecast under the amount you plan to "Push" or "Pull", you won't have enough finished goods to send to the regional warehouses. If you forecast over the amount, you're leaving finished goods in your main warehouse. No customer can purchase from your main warehouse, and too many finished goods leads to additional warehouse expenses.

Watch your sales forecast! Adjust as necessary.

FAQ

When I transfer inventory to a storage location, am I charged €1,000 per product, per location?

You are charged €1,000 each time you transfer any quantity of any combination of finished products from the main warehouse to the regional storage location. It is €1,000 regardless of how much or how little you send.

What is the capacity when shipping to a regional storage location?

There is no capacity for shipping between the main warehouse and the regional storage locations. You are able to transfer as much as or as little as you'd like each time you send finished products to a storage location.

How do I move inventory from one regional storage location to another?

You cannot move inventory from one regional storage location to another. Keep this in mind when planning your strategy. If you send too much and it doesn't sell... it's stuck there.

Are shipments to regional storage locations consolidated?

Yes, every time you ship the allocated finished products to a regional storage location, all scheduled products will ship at once. You will be charged €1,000 per shipment regardless of how much or how little you send.

How do I increase warehouse capacity?

Within the ERPsim Manufacturing Game, your warehouse capacity is automatically increased once you exceed your warehouse capacity. Check the job aid for these associated costs.

Remember that your regional storage locations are rented storage locations following the same daily costs as listed on the job aid under "storage capacity and costs".

Relevant Information Form

For Labs 01 through 03

SAP Lab 01

Line	Description	Your Information
1.1	PO Amount – Foodbroker Inc.	
1.2	PO Number – Foodbroker Inc.	
1.3	PO Amount – Continental Printing	
1.4	PO Number – Continental Printing	
1.5	Planned Order Number	
1.6	Production Order Number	

SAP Lab 02

Line	Description	Your Information
2.1	Order's Total Net Value	
2.2	Standard Order #	
2.3	Outbound Delivery #	

SAP Lab 03

Line	Description	Your Information
3.1	Accounting Invoice Number	
3.2	2.1 – (1.1+1.3) Sales Order – Total Raw Materials	Net from **Sales – Production**

Forgot to write something down? Need to double-check a value?
For lines 1.1 through 1.4 use SAP transaction code ME23. Lines 1.5 and 1.6 should be within MD04. For all of Lab 02 and line 3.1, use SAP transaction code VA03 (use the document flow for all subsequent documents). You will need to search for your document/order/value within each transaction. Look online for transaction instructions, or click around until you find what you're after. An incorrectly submitted document or order should be replaced.